1000 Best Casino Gambling Secrets

Bill Burton

Published by Sourcebooks, Inc.
P.O. Box 4410, Naperville, Illinois 60567-4410
(630) 961-3900
FAX: (630) 961-2168
www.sourcebooks.com

ISBN-13: 978-1-4022-0515-6

Library of Congress Cataloging-in-Publication Data
Burton, Bill.
   1000 best casino gambling secrets / Bill Burton.
      p. cm.
   Includes index.
   ISBN 1-4022-0515-5 (alk. paper)
   1. Gambling. 2. Casinos. I. Title: One thousand best casino gambling secrets. II. Title.

GV1301.B87 2005
795—dc22

                                              2005020140

Printed and bound in Canada.
WC 10 9 8 7 6 5 4 3 2

Dedication

To Miriam and Bob Convertito
The best of friends and fellow casino warriors.

1000 Best Casino Gambling Secrets

Bill Burton

SOURCEBOOKS, INC.®
NAPERVILLE, ILLINOIS

Table of Contents

Acknowledgments

My biggest concern in writing the acknowledgments for this book is possibly leaving out someone whom I should mention. I apologize if I have inadvertently left anyone out. All I can say is, you know who you are, and I appreciate your help.

Over the years, I have had the opportunity to meet and become friends with some of the most knowledgeable experts and writers in the gaming world. We have discussed, and at times debated, all aspects of the games and casino industry while readily sharing our ideas and knowledge. We have learned from each other along the way.

I want to say thanks to some of the people who have helped me by sharing not only their expertise but also, more importantly, their friendship through the years. Frank Scoblete, Henry Tamburin, Jean Scott, Don Catlin, Skip Hughes, and John Grochowski are a few of the country's top gaming authors whom I have the privilege of calling friends.

I want to thank Howard Schwartz and Maryann Gubermann at the Gambler's Book Shop in Las Vegas for being so generous with their time and help whenever I visit Las Vegas.

I want to thank Bethany Brown, Senior Editor at Sourcebooks, for getting this project started. I owe a big "Thank You!" to Ewurama Ewusi-Mensah and Rachel Jay, my two editors, who spent their time editing this book, giving it the polish it needed, and keeping me on track when I got a little too technical with my terminology. Thanks to Barb Doyen, my agent at Doyen Literary Services, for bringing me this project.

I want to thank my Golden Touch craps partners who have made playing craps both enjoyable and profitable. Also for sharing your wisdom and advice: Bob, Dominator, Jerry, Billy, Street Dog, Howard, Arman, Daryl, Jake, Dave, and the rest—you guys are the best.

Last but not least, I want to thank my wife Sandy for her patience, understanding, love, and support during the writing of this book and through all our years together.

1.

Play like a Pro:
How Casinos are Run

THE BASICS

1. Luck comes and goes, but knowledge stays forever. If you want to play a game that requires skill, do your homework. Take the time to read about and practice the games you want to play before you sit down and risk money at the tables.

2. Never take money to the casino that you can't afford to lose. Most casino games have a "negative expectation": they are set up so that you will lose in the end. You should view your visit to the casino as entertainment; the money you gamble with is the price of admission.

3. Casinos are big business. Their business is to separate you from your money while you are having a good time. Keep in mind that the money that built those big resorts came from losers, and be aware of some of the ploys used by the casino to separate you from yours.

4. Always wear a wristwatch or bring a small watch with you. The casinos want you to lose track of time, which is why there are no clocks or windows in the gaming areas.

5. The carpets in the casinos are designed to keep you from looking down. They have patterns that are meant to cause you to turn your eyes away and keep you looking straight ahead at the machines and the tables.

6. When you enter the casino, look around for something to use as a landmark to help you find your way. Many casinos are designed to be confusing to keep guests wandering around and playing along the way.

7. The casinos use a sophisticated surveillance system to detect cheating or security problems. They have video cameras in the ceiling to monitor all the games and action in the casino. This is known as the "eye in the sky." Years ago the surveillance was done from scaffolds in the casino ceiling; security staff would look through peepholes and two-way mirrors to catch cheaters at work.

8. The casinos may have the house edge on all the games, but you have a big advantage over them: you can quit any time you want. Make sure to walk away with a profit when you are winning.

9. Casino games fall into two categories. They are either games of luck or games of skill. In games of luck, the house advantage is predetermined so success is out of your hands. With games of skill, players can make decisions that will affect the house advantage.

10. Many casinos offer free lessons for table games such as craps or blackjack. Taking a lesson is a good way to learn the mechanics of the game, and some casinos give players match play coupons or other incentives to take lessons.

11. You can learn the strategy for blackjack and video poker on your home computer with the help of tutorial software. Spending your money on a program to learn to play at home is cheaper than trying to get your education at the gaming table.

12. Many recreational players either will not take the time to learn correct playing strategies or will choose to ignore them and play by intuition. To play smart and win you have to believe in the math of the game and apply the best strategy possible. The casino does not rely on luck or hunches to achieve their edge and neither should you.

13. Nobody plans to lose, but losers fail to plan. In addition to knowing how to play each game, winning players need to make a game plan for their time in the casino. Decide ahead of time what games you want to play and the amount of money you plan to risk.

14. Gambling is about risk and reward. Usually the bigger the reward you seek, the more you have to risk to get it. Generally, the casino will have a greater house edge on bets that offer the biggest jackpots.

15. Your emotional bankroll is the amount of pressure you can stand while you gamble; some players can't handle the pressure of large bets even if they can afford the financial loss. You should never bet more than your emotional bankroll can handle. If the size of your bet makes you nervous, it is too big. Lower your bet.

16. The colors of chips are standard in most casinos. This is so the pit personnel or "eye in the sky" can quickly determine the amount that is being bet. The most popular colors used for chips are:

White or Blue: $1
Red: $5; called "nickels"
Green: $25; called "quarters"
Black: $100
Purple: $500; called "Barneys"
Orange: $1000; called "pumpkins"

17. All table games have a placard located somewhere on the table that will tell you the minimum and maximum bets. Some placards are color-coded to correspond to chips for that limit. For example, five-dollar tables will have a red card and twenty-five-dollar tables will have a green card. Always look for these before sitting down.

18. Casinos prefer that players use chips to place bets, but most casinos will allow you to make a single bet by putting cash on the table. The dealer will call out, "Money plays" to signify to the floor that the cash on the table is a bet. If you are making more than one bet, they will ask you to convert your cash into chips. If you want to use traveler's checks, you will need to convert them to cash at the casino's cashier cage.

19. Dealers are not allowed to take money directly from your hands. To purchase chips, place your money on the table. The dealer will pick up your money and count it in plain view of the surveillance cameras. He will then push you your chips.

20. Dealers cannot convert your chips into cash when you get done playing. You will have to take them to the cage. When you are ready to leave the table, tell the dealer you want to "color up," and he or she will convert your low denomination chips to higher denomination chips.

21. The casino encourages the player to color up when leaving the table for two reasons. One is for the player's convenience as it makes them less likely to drop chips on the way to the cage. More importantly, it lets the casino know exactly how much the player has won or lost.

22. Players are not allowed to use chips from other casinos to gamble. As a courtesy to the players, many casinos will exchange the chips from neighboring casinos at the casino cage. Dealers are not allowed to do this at the table.

23. Don't gamble if you are angry or upset. You should always be thinking clearly if you are going to gamble, and you should never take your emotions out on the dealer.

24. Be realistic about your expectations. You won't turn $100 into a million. Be happy with small wins and know when to walk away.

25. Nobody likes a know-it-all. Don't give unsolicited advice to other players at the gaming table. Remember that the other player is using his money, not yours. He can play any way he wants.

26. American casinos do not have dress codes, and you can wear casual clothes. European casinos, on the other hand, do enforce a dress code. Be aware of this if you are traveling abroad and plan to visit a casino.

Who's Who in the Casino

27. It is no secret that organized crime ran casinos many years ago. This is not the case anymore. Casinos are now controlled by large corporations, the majority of which are publicly traded on the New York Stock Exchange and many of which run major hotel operations as well. Today, the larger casinos employ hundreds or even thousands of employees with an upper management similar to that of other major corporations with a board of directors, CEO, CFO, and president.

28. Most states with legalized gaming, particularly the major jurisdictions such as Nevada, New Jersey, Connecticut, and Mississippi, have a state regulatory body, commonly called the Casino Control Commission, which oversees the casinos and the games. To avoid being cheated, you should only play in casinos that are governed by these state agencies.

29. Any new game or change in an existing game must be approved by the Casino Control Commission in states where gambling is regulated. New slot machines must be tested in a lab and then field-tested before they are approved. This is to assure that the player and the casino get a "fair game."

30. The vice president of casino operations is usually the senior executive who is in charge of the overall business affairs of the casino. He or she will report directly to the president. The VP is in charge of the casino manager and other departments that affect the business side of the casino.

31. The casino manager is the person who runs the day-to-day casino operation. The casino manager is responsible for setting the procedures and policies concerning the games, scheduling, table limits, personnel, and training. Many of the casino managers have come up through the ranks and know every detail of every aspect of the casino business. The casino manager may have an assistant to handle affairs in his or her absence.

32. Each shift manager or boss oversees the operations on the day, night, or graveyard shift and makes the decisions affecting the personnel on his shift. The casino manager is usually in the office handling administrative matters, but you can find the shift manager on the floor handling any issues that might arise. There is always a shift manager on duty any time of the day or night.

33. The table games in the casino are arranged in an area called the pit. Each pit has a pit boss who is responsible for overseeing the games in that pit. They assure that the games are conducted according to the rules and oversee all employees and players in the pit to make sure all procedures and policies are followed.

34. There are several floor persons in each pit who assist the pit boss and directly monitor the dealers at their assigned tables. They are in charge of watching the dealers and rating the players. They oversee the transactions when the players buy their chips and when the dealers pay money to the winning players.

35. The dealers are the front line to any casino operation. They are responsible for dealing the game in accordance with the casinos policies, handling the player's money, and treating the players in a friendly and courteous manner.

36. The slot supervisor is to the slot department what the pit boss is to table games. They oversee the slot attendants and technicians to make sure everything related to the slot operation is running smoothly.

37. The slot attendant is the person you call when you have a problem with the machine. He can fix minor problems or fill the hopper if needed. He is also in charge of delivering your money when you hit a jackpot that requires a hand pay.

38. A change attendant roams the casino floor making change and selling rolls of coins to the players. Change attendants are slowly being phased out as more and more casinos adopt the new ticket in-ticket out system.

39. The slot technician is the person who fixes the machines when the problem is more complex than the slot attendant can fix. Technicians are in charge of installing new machines on the slot floor and moving machines around when necessary.

40. The casino host works hand-in-hand with the marketing department to bring in players and keep them happy. Hosts can write comps for players for anything from a free meal to an all-expense-paid visit including food, room, and more. You don't have to be a high roller to ask a host for a comp, so go ahead and give it a try. The worst thing they can do is say "no."

41. Most casinos have two separate departments for security and surveillance. The surveillance employees are in charge of watching everybody in the casino. The security department employs the guards in charge of protecting the patrons and casino personnel.

2.

Great Expectations:
Odds, Probabilities, and House Edge

THE BASICS

42. Gamblers believe in luck. Casinos believe in math. Since there are many more millionaire casino owners than there are millionaire gamblers, we know who has the edge.

43. Probability is the mathematical likelihood of an event occurring. It is expressed as a percentage or a number between zero and one. The odds of something never occurring are zero and the odds of an event always occurring is one. For example, the probability of a coin landing on heads when flipped is 0.5 or 50 percent.

44. The casinos win in two ways. The first way is to offer games where the casino wins more decisions than the player does. The second is to charge players when they win by paying them less than true odds.

45. True odds are determined by the probability of an event occurring. The casinos pay you less than true odds when you win. The house edge is the difference between the true odds and the odds that the casino pays you when you win.

46. If you bet on the flip of a coin, the probability of heads or tails is fifty-fifty. This would be an even money bet. If you bet a dollar and were paid a dollar when you won, you would be paid true odds. However, if the casino only paid you ninety-five cents every time you won instead of a dollar, the house edge would be 2.5 percent.

47. Let's say a player flips a coin one hundred times and wagers one dollar on each flip. If he wins the toss, he wins ninety-five cents. If he loses the toss, he loses one dollar. After one hundred coin flips, here are the results:

He has won fifty times x ninety-five cents = +$47.50
He has lost fifty times x one dollar = -$50.00
The player's expected loss is $2.50 after wagering one hundred dollars, which translates to a negative expectation of $2.50/$100 x 100 = -2.5 percent.

48. The money it costs to play a game in relation to the house edge is called the expected value or EV. The EV is a percentage of the total money wagered that a player can expect to win or lose. It is the average of all the possible outcomes, referred to as the "long run."

49. All but a few casino games have a negative expected value, which means that you will lose over the long run. Since luck does figure in when playing casino games, it is possible to win in the short term. The longer you play, the more likely you will be to lose.

50. Standard deviation is the fluctuation that occurs between the probability of an event occurring and the actual outcome. It can be toward the positive side if an event occurs more than it mathematically should or the negative side if it occurs less than it should. The ebb and flow of positive and negative fluctuation is what we actually mean when we refer to luck.

51. Blackjack is in a different category from other casino games because every time a card comes out of the deck, it changes the makeup of the remaining cards. The advantage can shift from player to house depending on which cards have been dealt.

52. An even money bet pays you back the same amount that you wagered in addition to returning your original bet. So, if you bet one chip, you would end up with two; your profit is one chip.

53. One thing that separates gaming from other forms of entertainment is there is no set price you pay to play. When you go to a show, you know in advance the price of the tickets. When you sit down to try your luck in the casino, you don't know exactly how much it will cost you to play.

54. The best and worst bets in the casino are determined by the EV for the player. Since the majority of the casino bets have a negative EV, the ones with the lower house edge can be considered the best bets. The ones with the higher house edge are the worst bets.

Ten of the Best Casino Bets

55. Poker: Poker is a game of skill. The house has no advantage other than a small amount it rakes out of each winning pot. The players are competing against each other and skill is a big factor in determining the winner. (See Chapter 10 for more about poker.)

56. Sports Betting: Betting on sporting events is only legal in Nevada, but experienced handicappers can make money. The house collects only a small fee on losing bets. (The fee is called the vigorish or vig, for short.) The odds makers set lines on how they believe the public will bet (not necessarily which team they think is better) in an attempt to balance winning bets against losing bets. (See Chapter 13 for more about sports betting.)

57. Blackjack Card Counting: Learning to count cards can give the player a 1 to 2 percent edge over the casino. Card counting is a skill that takes time and practice to master. Counters must also learn how to disguise their skills at the table since they are not welcomed by casinos. (See Chapter 6 for more about card counting.)

58. Video Poker: Video poker is another game of skill that has a small house edge if you make the correct playing decisions. Some video poker games offer over 100 percent payback to players utilizing perfect mathematical strategy. Other video poker games have less than a one percent house edge when you play correctly. (See Chapter 5 for more about video poker.)

59. Blackjack Basic Strategy: Learning and playing blackjack basic strategy will lower the house edge to less than one percent. The house advantage over basic strategy players is 0.18 to 0.55 percent, depending upon the number of decks used and the casino rules. (See Chapter 6 for more about blackjack.)

60. Craps Don't Pass/Don't Come: The don't pass/don't come bet in the game of craps is just slightly better than the pass line bet. The house edge is 1.40 percent. You can lower this to .59 percent by laying double odds. Most players, however, like to bet with the shooter on the pass line. (See Chapter 7 for more about craps.)

61. Craps Pass Line/Come: The pass line and come bets in the game of craps offer a low house edge of 1.41 percent. You can lower it to less than one percent (.61) if you take double odds on your bet. (See Chapter 7 for more about craps.)

62. Pai Gow Banker: A player may choose to act as the banker during the pai gow game. If a player banks the game, a 5 percent commission is charged on the net win. Setting the hands requires skill, but a good player can gain an advantage that will lower the house edge below one percent. (See Chapter 9 for more about pai gow.)

63. Baccarat Banker/Player: The baccarat banker bet requires you to pay a commission on winning bets. The house edge is 1.06 percent for the banker bet. The player bet is also a good bet with a house edge of only 1.24 percent. (See Chapter 9 for more about baccarat.)

64. Craps Place Six and Eight: Placing the six and eight at the craps table is one of the best bets in the game. The house edge is only 1.52 percent. The six and eight are rolled more frequently than any number other than the seven. (See Chapter 7 for more about craps.)

Ten of the Worst Casino Bets

65. Caribbean Stud Side Bet: The side bet for the progressive jackpot in Caribbean stud varies a little by the size of the jackpot, but it rarely reaches the amount to make the bet worthwhile. The average house edge is about 26 percent. (See Chapter 9 for more about Caribbean stud.)

66. Live Keno: Keno is a game similar to the lottery. The house edge can run 25 percent or higher. The odds for drawing any number of spots doesn't change. The house edge comes from the payout for the winning numbers. This varies from casino to casino. (See Chapter 12 for more about keno.)

67. Big Six Wheel: The big six or wheel of fortunes is an old carnival game with equally bad odds. The house edge varies from 11 to 24 percent depending on the number the player bets. (See Chapter 9 for more about big six.)

68. Baccarat Tie: While the baccarat banker and player bets are the best, the tie bet in baccarat is one of the worst. It has a high 14.36 percent edge. Stick to the banker or player bets. (See Chapter 9 for more about baccarat.)

69. Blackjack Insurance: The insurance bet in blackjack is just another side bet that should be avoided. The house edge is around 8 percent. You are not really insuring anything. (See Chapter 6 for more about blackjack.)

70. Blackjack Hunch Play: Deviating from blackjack basic strategy can make blackjack one of the worst games in the casino. A player can give up 20 percent or more playing hunches. (See Chapter 6 for more about blackjack.)

71. Let It Ride Side Bet: The house edge for the side bet is based on the pay table, which varies from casino to casino. Even the best pay table has a high double-digit house edge that ranges from 13 to 36 percent. (See Chapter 9 for more about let it ride.)

72. Craps Proposition: The proposition bets on the craps table are the bets on the hard ways and the one roll bets. These have a house edge that can reach as high as 16.7 percent. (See Chapter 7 for more about craps.)

73. Roulette: The bets on the double zero American wheel have a house edge of 5.26 percent on all bets except the five number bet. The five number bet (0-00-1-2-3) is called the basket bet and has a house edge of 7.89 percent. The European wheel with a single zero has a lower house edge of 2.7 percent. (See Chapter 8 for more about roulette.)

74. Casino War Tie: There is a tie bet that can be made when playing casino war. You are betting that your card will tie the dealer's. If you win, you get paid ten to one for your bet. It carries a high house edge of 18.65 percent. (See Chapter 9 for more about casino war.)

75. A good rule of thumb is to realize the side bets on any casino games are sucker bets. All of them carry a high house edge. Sometimes players have an "it's only a dollar, so why not gamble" attitude. Remember that over the course of a year, those dollars add up and will cost you more than you think.

76. The speed of a game can hurt the player. The faster the game, the more your money is exposed to the house edge. Roulette has a high house edge, but if you play at a full table, you will only get about thirty decisions per hour.

77. Any new rule changes on existing casino games are not good for the player. They are made to increase the profits for the casino. Some casinos on the Las Vegas strip are paying six to five for a natural blackjack instead of three to two. This increases the house edge by 1.5 percent.

78. The average return on slot machines around the country is 92 percent. Some casinos have a few machines set to pay back 99 percent. Most states have laws that specify the minimum payback that the machines can be set to.

79. You have better odds of being struck by lightning than you do for winning one of the big progressive jackpots. Since a portion of the money played is allocated towards the progressive jackpot, the returns on these machines are even lower than the average. Unless you hit the big jackpot, you are just donating money to the eventual winner.

80. The game of sic bo is the equivalent to the big six wheel. It is a game played with three dice in a cage. Instead of betting on dollar denominations, you are betting on dice combinations. The house edge on some of these bets is as high as 48 percent.

3.

Dollars and Sense: Money Management

THE BASICS

81. It's easy to leave the casino when all your money is gone. It takes discipline to walk away when you are ahead. Discipline and control are what separate the winners from the losers. If you don't learn how to handle your money, the casino will do it for you once it becomes their money!

82. Many players win when they are playing and then give it all back. They rationalize that they were playing with the casino's money. Once you win a bet, it is your money, not the casino's money. You should treat it accordingly.

83. Churn is the term used for replaying your winnings. The casino is counting on you to churn your winnings because eventually they will get it all back. The house edge will slowly eat away your winnings as you replay them.

84. The goal of money management is to bet more when you are winning and less when you are losing. This is easier said than done as you never know that you are in a winning or losing streak until it ends.

85. Don't ever borrow money or take cash advances on your credit cards to use for gambling. The fees imposed when you use your credit card for a cash advance in the casino are huge. This is in addition to the fee charged by your credit card company.

86. Leave the checkbook, credit cards, and ATM cards at home. Taking a cash advance to play a negative expectation game is very costly, and you will lose more money than you planned to.

87. Casinos convert your money into chips when you play table games. They do this because they know you are less likely to think of the colored chips as money. Always remember that chips are real money.

88. Dollar slot players use tokens for the machines. Just like the chips, these tokens lose their value. If you were using silver dollars, you would hesitate a little more before randomly dropping them into machines. Think of the slot tokens as dollars because that's exactly how much they are worth.

89. The casino supplies you with free drinks, but don't drink alcohol when you gamble. It will loosen your inhibitions, and you are likely to bet more than you planned to.

90. Keep your gambling sessions short. You can win at casino games in the short term, but the longer you play, the more likely it is that the house edge will catch up to you.

91. Don't play at limits you can't afford. If you only have one hundred dollars, don't play at a twenty-five-dollar table or dollar slot machine. Your goal is to make your money last. One short losing streak will wipe you out if you don't have a sufficient bankroll. There is no shame in playing lower limit games.

92. Make sure you have sufficient funds with which to gamble. Being under-capitalized will force you to bet less than you would like to when you have the edge over the casino. For example, if you are playing blackjack and strategy calls for you to double down, you may not do it because you are short on money. This will cost you money.

93. Maintain a separate gambling bank account. This is money used only for your casino visits throughout the year. You can set aside a few dollars each week and before you know it, you will have built yourself a nice-sized gambling account.

94. Many casinos are converting to coinless slot machines that require you to put dollars in a bill receptor. Put in only half the amount of your session budget. For example, put in ten dollars if you brought twenty. If you lose it quickly, you can switch machines or take a break. Never put in a higher denomination than you can afford to lose.

95. The ticket out system was designed to get players to play off a few credits rather than walking to the cage to collect a small amount of money. Keep in mind that playing off a dollar here and there adds up to a lot of money over the course of your casino visits.

96. Savor a win. There is nothing better than the feeling of walking away a winner. If you are ahead after playing for a few hours, take a break and enjoy your win. You can always go back to the games later.

Betting Systems

97. There are many betting systems you can use. Ideally, you should pick one and stick to it for the complete session. It will not change the odds of any game, but a good system will help you control the amount of money that you put at risk. This will enable you to play longer on your bankroll.

98. The Martingale system involves doubling your bet after each loss. This is a dangerous system and many players have gone broke trying it. The casinos have a maximum bet on all the games and it only takes about eight losses in a row to reach it. Do not try this system.

99. The Labouchere is another dangerous negative progression system that should be avoided. It involves starting with a series of numbers that add up to your desired win, such as 1, 2, 3, 4, 5, 6. You start by adding the outside numbers (1 + 6 = 7) and you bet that. If you win, your next bet is 2 + 5. If you lose, you add one to the series and your next bet would be 1 + 7.

100. If you want to use a system, use a positive progression betting system. When you have won two bets, increase your bet by one half of a bet. Go back to the minimum when you lose. For example, if you are betting ten dollars a hand, collect on two wins, then increase your bet to fifteen dollars. If you lose that bet, you are still ahead by five dollars.

101. The Regression system involves reducing your bet after a win in order to take a profit even if you lose the next bet. It can be used along with the positive progression system. In the example above if you win your $15 bet you can regress back to a $5 bet and have a $25 profit even if you lose. Another way to use the Regression is to make your first bet twice the size and regress back if you win.

102. The parlay bet is one of the oldest betting systems. It simply involves doubling your bet when you win. You are betting your winnings along with your initial bet. Many players refer to it as "double or nothing."

103. In a hedge bet, you make two offsetting bets to try to win a little. In sports betting, for example, if you bet a two-team parlay and you win on the first team, betting a smaller amount against the second team would allow you to recoup the amount of your original parlay bet if your second team loses or make a small profit if the parlay wins. Hedge betting is not to your advantage.

104. Don't purchase any betting systems through the mail or off the Internet. All mail order solicitations are basically the same. They are filled with hype to get you excited, but devoid of any real details. Many are just repackaged versions of existing betting systems such as the ones listed in this section.

105. The casinos love all system players except for card counters. Other than card counting in blackjack, there is not a system in the world that will change the house edge on any of the games. All a system will do is affect the short-term fluctuations of the payer's bankroll. The casino is open 24/7 and has an unlimited bankroll. They don't have to sweat the system player who has an occasional win.

106. Many betting systems do win more often than they lose. The problem is that the wins are small and the losses are big. With most systems, a single loss can wipe out a whole series of wins.

107. Beware the winning system! Casinos would love to have every player who devises a system to win the first few times they use it. Once a player feels that he has found the perfect system, that dangerous human emotion will kick in—greed. He will think his system is unbeatable and begin increasing his bets. The math of the game will finally catch up with him, and the casino will have their money back along with some of the player's money.

Simple Money Management Plan

108. Before you leave for vacation, decide exactly how much money you will spend on gambling. This gambling bankroll should be separate from your other spending money, and it must be money that you can afford to lose.

109. Divide your bankroll by the number of days you will be at the casino. Put each day's money in a separate envelope to be used for that day only. Break each day's casino bankroll down into several playing sessions. Don't risk it all at once, and be sure to take a break between sessions. At the end of each day, put all your winnings—or whatever money you have left—back in the envelope and seal it. You will take this money home with you.

110. Set a stop loss of half your session bankroll, and don't go past it during any of your playing sessions. If you reach it, take a break or try playing a different game. Leave your other money locked in your room safe or the casino safe. This way you won't be tempted to overspend your bankroll if you have a losing session.

111. If you can follow this plan, you will more than likely bring money home. If you have a couple of winning days and a couple losing days, it's possible that the wins will offset the losses. It takes discipline to seal up the money and not open the envelope, but in the long run, you will be happy you did.

Casino Credit

112. If you have the discipline, you can apply for casino credit. Call a few weeks before you visit the casino and speak to the casino cashier or cage. Ask them to send you a credit application that you will fill out and send back.

113. Once you have established credit, you will be given a line of credit. You can take "markers" up to your credit limit. When you sit down at the table, tell the floor person that you want a marker. In many casinos, you must request multiples of five hundred dollars.

114. A marker is essentially a loan from the casino. If you have a winning visit, it is customary to pay back all markers before you leave. If you don't pay them back you usually have fourteen to thirty days to pay depending on the casino policy.

115. In most casinos, your credit is tied directly to one of your bank accounts. If you do not pay back the marker by the allotted date, the money is withdrawn from your bank account. Your signed marker is essentially a bank check.

116. Casino credit is part of the customer service that is extended to the player by the casino. It increases player loyalty because you will be inclined to play at a casino where you have a line of credit. It is also a convenience for the player not to have to carry extra cash when visiting the casino.

117. When you establish a line of credit, the casino looks at your credit limit as the amount you are willing to risk. They tend to be a little more generous with comps when you have a credit line, so establishing a line of credit with the casino can increase your comp rating.

118. If you don't want to establish a credit line, you can still apply for check cashing privileges at the casino cage. This will allow you to bring a check with you instead of carrying cash to the casino.

119. Never apply for any casino credit if you don't have the discipline to control your gambling. Having credit can be a benefit, but it can also present big problems if you lose control. If you have any doubts about your ability to play within a budget, don't even think about casino credit.

120. WARNING! Failure to pay back a marker is a crime. It is just like stealing and the casinos will prosecute you if you skip out on your debts. Some players try getting higher credit limits by depositing a large sum of money in their bank account and then withdrawing it once their credit is established. Do not try this.

Keeping Records

121. If you are serious about your game, it is imperative that you keep a log detailing your wins and losses each time you play. If you play a game of skill such as poker or blackjack, you can use your logbook to assess your skills. Keeping records is the only way to tell if you are a winning player or not. It is not enough to rely on your memory if you want accuracy. Most players tend to remember the wins but forget about the losses.

122. If you are one of the "lucky" people who win money at the casino, you may find you aren't so lucky when you fill out your taxes. Uncle Sam loves to share in your joy by claiming a bite of your winnings for himself. That is exactly what happens each April 15 to many "winners" who don't keep a gambling diary or logbook.

123. When you win a jackpot over $1,200 on slot machines or have other big wins at keno or the racetrack, you will receive a W-2G form. A copy of this goes to the IRS and you are required to list these winnings when filing your income tax.

124. The law allows you to deduct gambling losses up to the amount of your winnings. You can only do this if you have documentation of your losses. Keeping a diary or logbook is the best way to do this, so your logbook must be accurate.

125. Your gaming log does not have to be fancy. You can keep it in a small notebook that you carry in your pocket. However, when you carry your log, you risk the chance of losing it. Many players write their daily play in the notebook and then transfer the information onto a spreadsheet on their computers.

126. A proper log must contain:

1) The type of game you played (slots, keno, craps, etc.)
2) The date and location where you played
3) Your wins and losses for each session or game
4) Additional evidence of gambling activities

127. Starting a log at the beginning of each year makes it a lot easier to keep track of all your gaming activities. Some players keep a separate log for each casino game they play. This way they know exactly where their gaming dollars are won or lost at a quick glance. It doesn't matter how you keep your log as long as you keep one.

128. If you use your player's cards, the casino has a record of your wins and losses. Most casinos will give you a printout if you request it. This may sound like the easy way out of keeping a log; however, it may not be accurate and it might not be accepted at tax time.

129. The government requires the casinos to report all cash transactions in excess of ten thousand dollars conducted by patrons in casinos. This is to alert them of possible money laundering or terrorism activities. Keep this in mind if you have a big win at the tables.

130. Generally speaking, keeping this type of log will be sufficient for tax purposes. However, you must be careful because tax codes do change. If you have a number of large wins, it would be wise to discuss this with a certified tax specialist, accountant, or lawyer. Don't take any chances that could put you in jeopardy with the government.

4.

Reel Fun: Slots

THE BASICS

131. Playing slot machines is the most popular form of gambling in the casino. Slot machines account for over 75 percent of most casinos' profits. The machines are programmed to hold a certain percentage of all money played through them.

132. The slot machine model that future slot machines would be based upon was invented in 1887 by Charles Fey in San Francisco. Fey's design featured three spinning wheels, each with ten symbols on it, including horseshoes, spades, diamonds, hearts, and bells. Lining up three bells won the jackpot.

133. Fey's machine would come to be known as the Bell machine. Because the machine had three reels with ten symbols on each, there were one thousand possible symbol combinations. The total payout for all winning combinations was 750 coins. This gave the house a 25 percent profit.

134. In later years, slots were disguised as vending machines because gambling was illegal. Bars with chewing gum logos were pictured on the reels, and the players would get a stick of gum or mints with their spin.

135. Modern day reel-type slot machines have a number of spaces on each reel that contain a symbol or blank. These are referred to as the physical stops. Most of the old mechanical machines had reels that could hold twenty symbols while the modern slots have reels with twenty-two physical stops, but hundreds of virtual stops.

136. In 1984, Inge Telnaes received a patent for his device titled, "Electronic Gaming Device Utilizing a Random Number Generator for Selecting the Reel Stop Positions." This device allowed for the creation of what we call the virtual reel. Microprocessing technology allowed the new machines to accommodate a large number of "virtual stops," which can number 256 or more. Each virtual stop was linked to one of the twenty-two physical stops on the reel.

137. In recent years, the slot makers introduced newer video slot machines, which are different from the slots with physical reels. With this technology and design, machines are not confined to having only twenty-two physical stops on each reel. The game designers can incorporate any number of video symbols on each reel, increasing the total number of combinations possible. This is the reason the video slots can offer such large jackpots.

138. The slot machines have a computer chip inside that runs the Random Number Generator (RNG), which selects the winning or losing combinations of numbers. The RNG is continuously cycling through numbers, even when the machine is not being played. These numbers correspond to the stops on the wheel that display the winning or losing symbols that you see when the reels stop.

139. The RNG uses a formula known as an algorithm, which is a series of instructions for generating the numbers. The scope of this is beyond most of our mathematical knowledge, but can be checked for accuracy. This is done by the casino control board and other testing laboratories to make sure that the program performs as it should so the player will not be cheated.

Types of Machines

140. Most people look at the vast array of slot machines at the casino and think that they are all alike. They see a handle, a coin slot, and flashing lights and assume one is as good as the next. Not all machines are the same and the way to separate one machine from another is to learn how to "read" a machine by looking at the machine's pay table.

141. The glass on the front of the slot machine contains information that will help you determine the type of machine. Listed on the glass will be the denomination of the machine and the pay schedule or pay table. The pay schedule will help you determine if the machine is a multiplier, progressive, or buy-a-pay machine.

142. The multiplier slot machine has a payout for each winning symbol, and the number of coins played multiplies this payout. If the machine pays five coins for three lemons when you play one coin, it would pay ten coins for the second coin played, and fifteen for three coins played. This machine does not penalize you for not playing maximum coins. If you plan to play only one coin at a time, this is the type of machine you should look for.

143. The bonus multiplier machine operates the same as the multiplier, except that it offers a bonus when you play maximum coins and hit the jackpot. Three sevens may pay one thousand for one coin, two thousand for two coins and ten thousand for maximum coins. You need to decide if the bonus is worth playing the extra coin. In most cases, you will want to play full coins in this type of machine.

144. The multiple pay line machines, which are becoming increasingly popular, have more than one line of play (the display of scrolling symbols). Each coin activates a particular line. If you hit a winner on a line that is not activated, you will not receive anything. They have nine or more lines and you can bet multiple coins on each line. You chose the number of lines you want to play and the number of coins for each line by pushing separate buttons. The reel type machines usually have a maximum of three lines.

145. The buy-a-pay are the most misunderstood machines in the casino. The number of coins played determines the winning symbols. You need the maximum coins to receive the largest jackpot. Don't play a buy-a-pay machine if you don't plan to play the maximum number of coins. If you hit the jackpot with one coin in, you will not win anything!

146. Progressive machines offer large jackpots. The big progressive jackpot is made by taking a percentage of all the money played into the machine. You can only win the progressive jackpot if you are playing the maximum number of coins. When you play a progressive with less than the maximum coins allowed, you are only building the jackpot for someone else.

147. To determine the payouts on a video slot machine, you will need to look at the help screen. If you are playing a game you have never played before, it is a good idea to spend a minute looking at the help screen so you understand the game. The help screen will show you what each symbol is worth and how they need to be aligned for you to win. It will also explain if there is a bonus screen for the game.

148. Many of the new video slots require that the winning symbols must start on the left reel and go to the right. You may line up three or four symbols in a row, but if they don't start in the first reel on the left, it is not a winner. You need to know this so you won't be confused as to why you did not win even though you had multiple symbols.

149. The lights on the top of the slot machines are called candles. The bottom light is colored and that color can tell you the denomination of the machine. In most cases, dollar machine candles are blue, quarter machine candles are yellow, and nickel machine candles are red.

150. Slow down when you are playing slot machines. There are no prizes for the player hitting the spin button the fastest. You will lose less money if you play more slowly.

151. Don't play more than one machine at a time. Playing more than one machine just leaves you more exposed to the house edge. In the long run, you will just lose your money more quickly.

152. If you like to hop from machine to machine, make sure you take your coin cup with you. Sometimes players will leave a machine in a hurry and forget their money. If you leave your change and walk away, chances are it will be gone by the time you go back to retrieve it. When you take your player's card out of the machine, make it a habit to put it into your coin cup. This way you won't forget to take it with you.

153. If you play the new ticket out machines, make sure to take your cash voucher. Some of the machines will beep loudly once the ticket is printed. You shouldn't depend on this because in a noisy casino you may not hear it. Make it a habit to reach for your ticket as soon as you hit the cash out button.

154. There will be times when a machine runs out of money and requires a hopper fill. You should stay by that machine until the attendant arrives. If you walk away, someone could sit down and claim that it is their money. Push the button to light up the change light. This will bring an attendant to the machine.

155. Reading the pay table of the machine can help you judge the frequency of winning spins. If you see a lot of combinations that return smaller wins, then this machine will usually have a larger hit frequency than one that has only a few large winning combinations. If you want to stretch your playing time, choose the machine with the higher hit frequency. This will give you a better chance of making your money last.

156. If you hit a jackpot, make sure that you "lock up" a profit. Take your initial playing stakes and some profit and set that money aside. Then play with a small percentage of your winnings. Depending on the size of the jackpot, I recommend no more than 25 to 30 percent. There is nothing worse than the feeling of being a winner and then giving all your winnings back to the casino.

157. Remember that credits on a slot machine are real money. Some players lose sight of this because the credits have no dollar amount attached to them. This makes it easy for some players to gamble with and lose their winnings.

158. Slot machines have a sign that says "malfunction voids all pays." If you feel that a machine has not paid you for a jackpot, call over a slot attendant immediately. They can have a technician run back the last few hands paid to see if there was a problem with the machine. You may get paid for your win after all.

159. Jackpots are paid by hand when they are too big for the machine's coin hopper to accommodate the coins. A quarter slot machine can usually payout 1,000 coins or $250. Anything more would require an attendant to bring you your winnings. On a dollar machine anything over $400 will usually require a hand pay.

160. When you hit a large jackpot, you will be required to show a photo ID. Have it ready for the attendant. They will check to make sure you are of legal age. If you are underage, the casino can deny you your winnings.

161. If you hit one of the big progressive jackpots that pays a million dollars or more, you will be paid in an annual annuity rather than a lump sum. This is great for the casino because they can retain the money from the jackpot and pay the player out of the interest they collect.

The Future

162. The innovative ticket in-ticket out system on the newer slot machines has been the most quickly accepted change in slots history. Players no longer have to handle dirty coins or wait for the hopper to be filled if the machine runs out of coins when they cash out. The system is also helping the casino cut costs. They no longer have to pay people to make change for players, empty coins from the machines, or count coins.

163. The new ticket system also makes it possible to offer the new penny slot games. These new games are multi-line, multi-coin games that would not be possible if they required jackpots to be paid out in actual coins. In January 2005, a man in San Diego, California won 2.1 million dollars on a penny progressive slot machine, which set a world record for penny slot machines.

164. Penny slots are the newest craze to hit the casino, but don't be fooled by the fact that you can bet pennies. All of these slots have multi-line games and a maximum bet on each line could cost you more than five dollars per spin.

165. There was a time when the casinos could expect to get a few years of play from each new machine they purchased. Now many of them come and go within a year to keep up with the demand for new games. This means that the player can expect to see newer and more exciting slots coming their way in the future.

166. It is only a matter of time before the spinning reel slot machine goes the way of their old mechanical predecessors. The new video slots have fewer moving parts that can break down. This makes them more dependable and easier to maintain.

167. Usually when you see a coin cup on a slot machine's handle or on the seat in front of the machine, it means that the machine is being played by another player. They could have run to the bathroom or gone to get change. You should respect this and look for another machine.

168. If you are the one holding the machine, then you should do what you have to do and get back to the machine as quickly as possible. In some casinos, if you need to take a bathroom break, you can ask a slot attendant to stand by your machine while you're gone. If you do have an attendant watch your machine, it is customary to tip them for doing so.

169. Some players who feel the need to play as quickly as possible like to use several machines at a time. During crowded times you should refrain from playing more than one machine and allow other players the opportunity to play. Some casinos have a sign stating "One machine per player during busy times."

170. If you are with a companion who is sitting next to you, but not playing, they should relinquish their seat if another player asks. Players can socialize later; the machines should be free for the players who want to play.

171. Sometimes a player will forget their player's card when they leave the machine. You will find it as you insert your card. It is customary to place the other player's card on top of the machine so that they can retrieve it later.

172. If you are a smoker in a casino that allows smoking, whenever possible, you should position your cigarette or ashtray in a way that minimizes the amount of smoke another player at an adjacent machine is exposed to.

Myths

173. If someone hits a jackpot on the machine you just left, he has not stolen your jackpot. If you had stayed at the machine, it is highly unlikely that you would have stopped the RNG at the exact millisecond to display that same combination of numbers. In the time it takes to talk with a friend or sip your drink, the RNG has cycled through thousands of combinations.

174. Casinos can't loosen or tighten the slot machines with the flip of a switch. The slot machines have a computer chip in them that determines the payback percentage. These are preset at the factory. In order for a casino to change the payback, they would have to change the chip. To change a chip the casino has to file paperwork with the Casino Control Commission for each machine they are changing.

175. There is no way to determine whether a machine is due to hit. Each spin is a random occurrence and has no bearing on what has happened previously. Never play more money than you should because of this myth. It will be devastating to your bankroll if you do.

176. Some players think that heating or cooling coins will lead to a jackpot. The machine is not affected by the temperature of the coins. It doesn't matter if you play hot, cold, old, or new coins. The coin slot is a mechanical device and has no feeling.

177. The winning symbols on a slot machine are controlled by the RNG. It does not matter if you hit the spin button or pull the handle. If you have a winning spin every time you use the handle and lose when you hit the button, it is only a coincidence.

178. You don't have to change machines when you hit a jackpot. The odds of hitting another jackpot on your next spin are the same as they were before you hit the jackpot. The payback percentages are programmed over the long run; anything can happen in the short run.

179. Some players refuse to use a player's card because they feel the machine will pay back less if they do. There is no link between the card reader and the RNG. By not using your player's card, you may be denying yourself valuable perks such as comps and cash back.

180. The number of coins you play does not affect whether the spin wins or loses. It will only affect the money you are paid.

181. You often hear players talk about machines having a cycle. The cycle just refers to all the combinations that can be made with the number of stops on the reels. It doesn't mean that if the jackpot is hit you have to wait until it picks all the other combinations before it will hit again.

182. Serious slots players should restrict their play to casinos in jurisdictions where slots results are published. This way they know the range of the slot payback. Play the highest denomination that you can afford, and play at casinos that offer the most generous comps.

183. Sometimes players are drunk or in a hurry and leave credits on the machine. In most jurisdictions if you find a machine that has credits on it, you can sit down and play. In some states, it is illegal to do this. Check the laws for the area where you play.

184. Some players will ask slot attendants to point out "loose slots" (the machines that frequently hit jackpots). Sometimes the attendants will offer to tell you without solicitation. If you do hit a jackpot after a recommendation, be prepared to give them a tip.

185. In the state of Nevada the regulations state that the credits that are left in a machine by a player technically belong to the casino. It is up to the casino to "prosecute" anyone found taking credits off a machine that don't belong to them. The reality is that the casinos don't prosecute unless the person willfully goes into a casino to check machines for credits left by other players and then takes them.

186. Slot machines in competitive markets have higher payback percentages. If there is only one casino or riverboat in your area, the payback will be lower. For your best chance of winning at slots, plan your visits to places that offer competition.

187. Some casinos will mark a bank of machines with signs pointing out the high payback for those machines. Look for the signs and read them carefully. It might say this machine pays back 99 percent or it could say some of the machines pay back 99 percent.

188. Play where the locals play. If you visit Las Vegas, get away from the strip and visit some of the other casinos frequented by area residents. The slots there usually have a better pay-back percentage because these casinos rely more heavily on business from the people living there.

189. Think like a casino executive. The casinos usually have both tight slots and loose slots which they position according to where they'll get the best return. Many players think that all the loose slots are placed by the entrances. This is not always the case.

190. Slot machines placed near the table games are usually tight. This is because many players will get up from the tables and be tempted to put spare change in the machines on their way to cash in their chips.

191. Many of the looser slot machines are found toward the back of the casino. The casino executives want to tempt you with the higher edge games along the way. Many players just want to play so they sit down at any machine, but you have to hunt for the loose machines.

192. Slot tournaments are becoming very popular. The main reason a casino holds a tournament is to attract players and generate additional business. They figure that while you are there waiting to play in the tournament, you will probably do a little playing on the side.

193. During a tournament, you are competing against the other players to see who can rack up the most credits on their slot machine. This means that, depending on the number of entrants, your odds may be better for winning a large amount of money compared to the normal return for slot machines or table games.

194. Some players enjoy playing tournaments because they know ahead of time what their potential losses will be. Since tournaments have a set entry fee, the participants know how much it will cost them to play. They can only lose the amount of their entry fee.

195. Not all tournaments are created equal. You will have to look at the prize structure and read the rules closely to determine if a tournament is a good deal for you. Tournaments fall into one of several categories: free, full, equity, invitational, and bad.

196. Free Tournaments: Some casinos offer free tournaments that are open to the public. They hold weekly or sometimes daily tournaments as a way to attract players into the casino. If you have never played in a slot tournament before, these free tournaments are an excellent way to find out if tournament play interests you.

197. Full Equity Tournaments: Many tournaments require the participants to pay an entry fee. The best-paid tournaments to enter are the ones that give back all the entry fees in the form of prizes. Casinos post the tournament rules and will list the prize structure with them.

198. Invitational Tournaments: Invitational tournaments are usually held as a reward or comp for loyal players. These are by invitation only and not open to the public. This is the ultimate comp for a slots player, as everyone usually walks away with some sort of prize. Some of these tournaments last two or three days and include free lodging.

199. Bad Tournaments: A bad tournament is one that the casino runs just to make a profit. They take a big portion of the entry fee, but offer little or no incentives in return for the player. If the casino takes any percentage of the entry fee and does not give you anything in return, you should pass on the tournament and look for one that offers you a fair return on your investment.

200. Some casinos offer a tournament package that will include additional incentives, freebies, and discounts. Some of these are discounted or free hotel rooms, a welcome party, an awards banquet, door prizes, and raffles. You should figure these additional benefits into your evaluation of the tournament.

201. Most tournaments have several qualifying rounds with the final event being held for all the players who advanced from the earlier rounds. You should look at the session times for the entire tournament before entering to determine if it fits into your schedule.

202. During a tournament, the time between the qualifying rounds and the final round can be several hours. This means that if you qualify, you are committed to staying at the casino while you wait for the final round. This might not be practical if you are on a tight schedule. The casinos plan it this way to get you to play while you wait. Watch your spending between rounds.

Tournament Strategy

203. Slot tournaments have a simple format. When you sign up for the tournament, you will be assigned a slot machine number and a session time to play. When it is your time, you find the machine with your number and have a seat.

204. A common format is to give each player one thousand credits with twenty minutes to play them. Each time you hit the spin button, the amount of credits for a maximum bet (usually three credits) is deducted from your starting credits. Any credits you win are shown on a separate meter. You do not get to replay any credits that you win.

205. When your time is up, the machine will lock up and play is over. Any credits that you have not played will be lost. The score on your winning meter will be compared to those of the other players to determine the winner.

206. After you finish playing, you wait at your machine until the official comes by and records your score. They will usually have you initial the results to verify that your score was recorded correctly. After your score is recorded, you will leave the machine.

207. In many tournaments, the highest scores are posted on a display near the tournament area. These are updated after each playing session. This allows you to judge how you are doing compared to the other players.

208. There is not a lot of strategy involved in winning a slot tournament. Luck is a big factor in deciding the winner. Speed and concentration can help you improve your chances.

209. Since you must play all your credits within a certain time, you must play fast enough to use all of them. Each winning spin will increase your total score. Any unused credits are lost and you will be at a disadvantage because you did not take as many spins as your opponents.

210. You can increase your speed by keeping your fingers on the spin button and continuously tapping it. Tap it lightly—you don't have to pound on the button. By leaving your fingers on it, you will save a few split seconds that you would have lost by taking your hand off the button.

211. Focus your concentration on hitting the spin button. Don't be distracted or spend time celebrating if you have a big hit. If you hit a big win, it will take a few seconds for the meter to register the credits. You can take a quick break, but you must be prepared to start tapping as soon as this is done.

212. Some players get tired or bored when they are playing in a tournament. This can cause you to slow down. Make sure you are fully rested before playing in the tournament. If you get bored easily, tournaments may not be for you.

213. Have fun! Tournaments are fun for players with a competitive spirit, but they are not right for everyone. If you are not competitive by nature, you may not enjoy tournament play.

5.

In Search of the Royals: Video Poker

THE BASICS

214. Video poker is based on the game of draw poker and has virtually the same rules except that you are not playing against any other players. The machine deals five cards on the screen. The player then has the option of drawing up to five new cards with the goal of creating a winning poker hand.

215. Video poker is a game of skill. The decisions that a player makes have an effect on the outcome of the game; making correct strategy decisions will improve your chances of winning. In most casinos, video poker machines offer a lower house edge than the slot machines when played correctly.

216. Video poker bridges the gap between the table games and the slot machines. Some players are intimidated by the table games, but want more than just the mindless spinning of reels they find on the slot machines. For these players, video poker is the answer.

217. When video poker machines first appeared on the casino floors in the late 1970s, the only game offered was jacks (or better draw) poker. Over the last few years, video poker has increased in popularity, and the casinos are adding more machines to the gaming floor. Today there are over one hundred variations of the game.

218. Many players who switch from the slot machines to video poker never go back again. They enjoy the challenge and the excitement of playing a game that requires a little skill. But don't let that scare you. Video poker is not hard to learn, and it is a lot of fun.

219. After being dealt your five cards, you keep the cards you want by pushing the "hold" button that corresponds to the card on the screen. When you have made your choice, you hit the "deal" button and the cards you discarded will be replaced by new cards. Your win or loss is determined by the outcome of your final hand after you hit the "draw" button.

220. Be careful using the hold button. Some players go so fast that when they hit the button, it does not register. Then they hit the deal button only to realize they threw away a card they wanted to keep. Make sure the cards you want to keep are held before hitting the deal button.

221. Don't automatically hit the maximum coin button. There was a time when the maximum bet on a video poker machine was five coins. Some of the newer machines have a maximum bet of ninety coins. You should check the help screen before hitting the max bet button so that you are certain what the maximum bet is.

222. The odds of making a video poker hand are identical to the odds if you were dealt a hand with a shuffled deck in a live game. The casino gains an edge in video poker by adjusting the payout for the different poker hands in relation to the odds of making that hand.

223. There are 2,598,960 hands that can be produced with a fifty-two-card deck. The RNG (random number generator) in video poker machines is set to simulate the probabilities of drawing any one of the combinations of hands in a deck dealt by hand.

224. There are software programs, strategy cards, books, and Internet sites where you can obtain the information you need to determine the payback percentage for each pay table. Knowing how to read a pay table can help you make sure you are playing the machine with the best return.

225. Unlike slot machines, there is no such thing as a loose video poker machine. The random number generator deals hands based on the true odds. A machine is not "programmed" to hit more or fewer royal flushes. The RNG is constantly dealing hands, even when no one is playing.

226. Nobody can steal your royal flush. If you get up and the next player sits down and hits a royal, it is highly unlikely that you would have hit it if you kept playing, because you would not have hit the deal button at the exact same millisecond.

227. The number of coins you play does not effect whether you win or lose. Although some machines deal the cards automatically when the fifth coin is inserted, it is no different from hitting the draw button with one coin in. It will not change the outcome of the hand.

228. Hold all five cards if you are dealt four-of-a-kind in jacks or better or non-wild games. This will minimize any chance of a machine malfunction. If you will not get any additional payout for drawing a fifth card, then don't.

229. The creators of video poker did something that no other gambling-game developer has ever been able to do: they made a push (tie) seem like a win. In most video poker machines, a pair of Jacks or better returns your original wager, and even though it's a push, it still feels like a win.

230. A tie is a win in video poker if you belong to the casino's players club. You get credit for coins being played through the machine. Since a tie returns your original bet, you can play it through again for more credit on your player's card.

231. Always check the pay table of the video poker machine before you sit down to play. A machine that pays the maximum return for a particular game is referred to as a "full pay" machine. You should memorize the full pay schedule of the video poker games you play so you know you are playing the one with the best possible return. In order to achieve the highest payback percentage, you must be playing maximum coins to get the bonus payout that is offered when you hit the royal flush.

232. The royal flush accounts for about 1.98 percent of all the money paid out over the long run. When you do hit the royal, the big jackpot will make up for a lot of your smaller losing sessions.

233. The reason that the casino can offer a game with over 100 percent payback is simple. Very few players take the time to learn to play perfect strategy. The number of hunch players who give the house a higher return more than makes up for the small percentage of expert players who play flawlessly.

234. You will have more losing sessions than winning ones. The key for the occasional player will be the frequency of the four-of-a-kind (odds: one in 423) and full houses (odds: one in eighty-six). If the frequency is above the norm, you will more than likely have a winning session; if you don't hit your fair share, you will probably lose.

235. The chance of hitting a royal flush when playing jacks or better is about one in forty thousand. That does not mean that you are guaranteed to hit a royal if you play forty thousand hands. The odds are the same each time you hit the deal button. You could hit a royal in one hand or go two hundred and fifty thousand hands without one.

236. The average person plays at a speed of around three or four hundred hands per hour. At four hundred hands per hour, it will take you about one hundred hours to play forty thousand hands. If you play four hours a day, it will take you twenty-five days. For the occasional visitor to the casino, it could take quite a few trips before you play the forty thousand hands.

237. Always play maximum coins to take advantage of the added jackpot for the royal flush. You are throwing money away for the bonus if you don't. If you can't afford to play maximum coins at the dollar level, drop down to quarters. If you can't afford quarters, drop down to nickels.

238. If you hit the royal flush on a quarter machine playing one coin (twenty-five cents) you will win $67.50. If you hit the royal flush on a nickel machine playing five coins (twenty-five cents) you will be paid $200. That is a difference of $132.50 for the same risk of twenty-five cents.

239. Playing maximum coins on a quarter machine will cost you $1.25 per hand. To play forty thousand hands, you will be putting fifty thousand dollars through the machine. If you play perfect strategy and hit the royal in forty thousand hands, you will achieve the 99.5 percent return. Your cost for playing the hands will be $50,000 x .05 percent or $250.

240. The advice for playing maximum coins is for a player who knows the correct strategy. If you are new to video poker and have no idea about correct strategy, then you will lose less if you play only one coin.

241. If you absolutely must play less than maximum coins on a video poker machine, then you should play a single coin. Don't play two, three, or four coins. Playing expert strategy with a single coin, you are playing almost even to the return, except for the bonus you get on the royal flush.

242. By using your player's card, you can recoup some of the cost of your play in comps. Some casinos offer cash back as well. The comps you receive can make up for a half percent of the house edge and turn a negative game into a positive one for the player.

243. The recreational or occasional player should be aware that it could take quite a long time to reach the theoretical return. Some players will never play enough to reach that goal. Learning and playing the correct strategy will help improve your chances of stretching you bankroll between royal flushes.

244. Some casinos will put two identical machines that have different pay tables next to each other. You want to make sure you are choosing the one with the highest return. Don't assume that the machines are identical because they are the same game and made by the same manufacturer. Read the pay table.

245. "Jacks or better" is the most common video poker game and there are several different pay tables for this game. When players refer to this game, they usually will denote the coins paid for the full house and the flush. If a machine pays nine coins for the full house and six coins for the flush, it is called a 9/6 jacks game. If it paid six for the full house and five for the flush, it would be called a 6/5 machine. Always play the machine offering the highest payback.

246. Learn to play jacks or better perfectly before moving on to the other variations of video poker games. This is the easiest game to learn, and it is the basis for many of the other games. The full pay 9/6 jacks or better game offers a payback of 99.5 percent.

247. In order to achieve the maximum return, you must play the game using a set mathematical strategy. It is very important that you learn the strategy for each game and play them correctly. Making a few mistakes in strategy when playing can increase the house edge against you. Each video poker game has its own strategy.

248. The optimal basic strategy of each game changes when the pay table changes. Make sure you are playing the correct strategy for the game you choose. The strategy for a 9/6 jacks or better game will differ from the optimal strategy of the 6/5 jacks or better game.

249. Winning hands for video poker games are based on the hierarchy of poker hands that you find in a live poker game. Only the payout for the highest hand is paid. The winning hands for a jacks or better machine are as follows.

250. Royal Flush: This is the best poker hand. It consists of a ten (T), Jack (J), Queen (Q), King (K), and Ace (A) of the same suit. The odds of making a royal flush are forty thousand to one.

251. Straight Flush: Five cards of the same suit that are in sequence. Example: six of hearts, seven of hearts, eight of hearts, nine of hearts, ten of hearts. The odds of making a straight flush are ten thousand to one.

252. Four-of-a-Kind: Four cards of equal rank. Example: Queen of clubs, Queen of hearts, Queen of diamonds, Queen of spades. The odds of making a four-of-a-kind are 423 to one.

253. Full House: Three cards of equal rank and two other cards of equal rank. Example: nine of hearts, nine of diamonds, nine of spades, five of clubs, five of diamonds (three-of-a-kind and a pair). The odds of making a full house are eighty-six to one.

254. Flush: Five cards of the same suit. Example: Ace of spades, ten of spades, nine of spades, seven of spades, and five of spades. The odds of making a flush are ninety-three to one.

255. Straight: Five cards of mixed suits, in sequence. Example: five of clubs, six of diamonds, seven of spades, eight of hearts, and nine of clubs. The odds of making a straight are eighty-five to one.

256. Three-of-a-Kind: Any three cards of equal rank. Example: eight of diamonds, eight of spades, and eight of clubs. The odds of making three-of-a-kind are thirteen to one.

257. Two Pairs: Two cards of equal rank and two other cards of equal rank. Example: King of clubs, King of spades, eight of diamonds, eight of spades. The odds of making two pairs are eight to one.

258. High Pair: This pair is a winning hand. Two Jacks, two Queens, two Kings, and two Aces are the four high pairs. The odds of making a high pair are five to one.

259. The joker poker game uses one or two jokers as wild cards. With the added wild cards, the lowest winning hand is higher than a pair of Jacks. In some games, you need a pair of Kings or better to get paid. Other games require two pairs or better. There are additional payouts added to the top including five-of-a-kind and a wild royal flush (a royal flush that uses a wild card).

260. In deuces wild, the twos are wild cards. The second best hand, after a royal flush is four deuces (or four twos), followed by five-of-a-kind and a wild royal flush. To make up for the wild cards, you need a three-of-a-kind or better to make a winning hand.

261. Full pay deuces wild offers a 100.7 percent return. The key to the return is the five coins paid for the four-of-a-kind. Some pay tables reduce the four-of-a-kind payout to four coins, decreasing the overall return by a whopping 6.4 percent. This is quite a reduction in the overall return. Always look for the machine that pays five coins for four-of-a-kind when playing deuces wild.

262. Double bonus poker is another game that offers a return of over 100 percent with proper play. The game pays double what standard bonus poker pays for four-of-a-kinds and gives you an extra coin for the straight. To make up for this additional bonus, the two pair payout is reduced to one coin. The key to adjusting the over-all return still lies in the payout of ten coins for the full house and seven coins for a flush.

263. If you are dealt four deuces in a game of deuces wild, you should hold all five cards. There is no way to improve this hand.

264. Video poker can be the best game in the casino, but it can also be the worst game if a player relies strictly on hunches to make decisions. The goal of most players is to learn to play perfect strategy, but even a simple game plan like the novice and intermediate strategies below will greatly improve your chances of winning on any jacks or better video poker pay table.

Novice Strategy

265. A pat hand is a winning hand that is dealt to you. Many pat hands require no thinking at all. Keep all five cards if you are dealt a royal flush, straight flush, four-of-a-kind, full house, or flush. The exception is to break up a flush or a straight if you have four cards of a royal flush. Then you would draw one card to try for the royal flush.

266. Do not break a straight flush. If you are dealt a straight flush that is nine through King of the same suit, you might be tempted to try for the royal flush; however, it's not worth breaking up this hand. Take the straight flush payout instead of trying for a royal.

267. If you are dealt three-of-a-kind, draw two cards. This will give you a chance at four-of-a-kind or a full house. If you are dealt two pairs, discard the fifth card for a chance at a full house.

268. If you are dealt a high pair, break up the pair only if you have a one-card draw to a royal or straight flush, that is, if drawing one more card could possibly give you a royal or straight flush. Many players make the mistake of breaking up a high pair for a simple flush. This is wrong and you should take the win for the high pair.

269. Keep a small pair over a single high card. A small pair can turn into two pairs, three-of-a-kind, four-of-a-kind, or a full house. Unlike a high pair, you should break up a small pair if you have a one-card draw to any flush.

270. An open-ended straight draw is one that can be made with a card on either end such as five, six, seven, eight. You have eight ways to complete the straight with one of the deck's four fours or one of the deck's four nines. An inside straight needs a card in the middle such as five, seven, eight, nine. Only four cards will make a straight in this situation (6 of diamonds, 6 of clubs, 6 of hearts, or 6 of spades). That is why you never draw to an inside straight in jacks or better.

Intermediate Strategy

271. The intermediate strategy is for players who want to improve their chances and reduce the house edge further than they would by using the novice strategy. It is a little more complex, but it is more accurate.

272. Use the chart below to find the best play for the hand you are dealt.

Your Hand	Recommended Play
Pat Hand	Keep all five
Four-Card Royal	Draw 1
Three-of-a-Kind	Draw 2
Four-Card Straight Flush	Draw 1
Two Pairs	Draw 1
High Pair	Draw 3
Three-Card Royal	Draw 2
Four-Card Flush	Draw 1
Small Pair	Draw 3
Open-Ended Straight	Draw 1
Three to a Straight Flush	Draw 2
Two-Card Royal—No Ten	Draw 3
Inside Straight—Three High Cards	Draw 1
Three High Cards—No Ace	Draw 2
Three-Card Straight Flush	Draw 2
Two High Cards	Draw 3
One High Card	Draw 4
Mixed Low Cards	Draw 5

273. Break any pat hand except a straight flush if you have a one-card draw to a royal flush. The payout for the other pat hands in relationship to the high payout for the royal makes this the best play.

274. Only break a high pair to draw to a four-card straight flush. Don't break a pat straight or flush. The difference in payoff between a royal and a straight flush makes keeping the pat hand a better choice.

275. Break up a four-card flush or open-ended straight to draw two cards if you have three cards to a royal flush. Break up a low pair to draw to a three card royal. Don't break a high pair.

276. Don't try to make a flush by drawing to three suited cards (that is, cards of the same suit) if they are not royal cards or there is not a chance to make an inside straight flush. The high odds against making a flush are such that this is not worthwhile unless you have a straight or royal draw.

277. Don't draw to an inside straight unless it contains three unsuited high cards. If you have a combination of two cards that includes Ace, King, Queen, or Jack along with a ten, then draw one to the inside straight.

278. Break up the four cards Ace, King, Queen, and Jack only if you have a suited Queen and Jack. If any other two-card combination is suited, keep all four cards.

279. If you have three unsuited high cards and one is an Ace, throw the Ace away. This gives you a better opportunity to make three-of-a-kind, two pairs, or four-of-a-kind. Only keep an unsuited Jack, Queen, and King.

280. Keep a suited ten if you have only a Queen or a Jack to go with it. If you have both a Queen and Jack, the better play is to keep them and discard the ten. Keep the King with a suited ten only if you don't have to discard a card of the same suit.

281. If you are not a frequent video poker player, you don't have to worry about memorizing the correct strategies. There are video poker strategy cards that you can purchase and take to the casino with you, or you can take this book along.

282. You can find video poker strategy charts for three of the most popular games: jacks or better, deuces wild, and double bonus poker on the Internet at: www.casinogambling.about.com/od/videopoker. To read the charts, start at the top and read down until you find the hand you were dealt.

283. You can learn to play video poker at home on your computer by investing in tutorial software. There are two excellent programs on the market: Bob Dancer Presents Winpoker and Jean Scott's Frugal Video Poker. These programs let you learn as you play by alerting you when you make a mistake. They come with over twenty different versions of video poker games.

284. Both Winpoker and Frugal Video Poker let you enter in a pay table and the program will calculate the return for that game. Frugal Video Poker even lets you print strategy cards that you can take to the casino with you. The money you spend on a software program will be recouped on the money you save by playing video poker correctly, and they are fun to use as well.

More Important Tips

285. Some video poker games have a double down option. After you win a hand, the machine will ask if you would like to double your win. If you choose to do this, you will be dealt five cards face down. You pick one and then the machine turns up one card. If your card is higher than the machine's, you double your win. If it's lower, you lose your winnings.

286. If you win your double down, you can elect to keep doubling until you decide to stop or you lose. The first time you double down, the odds are fifty-fifty that you will be able to double your money. When you attempt four doubles in a row, the odds drop to 6.25 percent.

287. Some players believe the myth that the machine knows when you are attempting to double a big win and will cause you to lose. This is not true. What is true is the fact that each time you double down, you are bucking the odds. You should avoid playing the double down bet.

288. Machines that have the double down option play more slowly because they ask you after each win if you want to double down. If you have no desire to double, you can ask a slot attendant to turn off the double down feature. Most casinos will honor your request to turn it off.

289. Progressive video poker machines are those that have a bonus payout for certain hands. Several machines are linked together and a percentage is taken from the play and added to a bonus pool, which is then awarded to the players who hit that particular hand. The most common is a bonus for the royal flush; however, some progressives also give bonuses for other hands such as a straight flush or four-of-a-kind.

290. To make up for a progressive bonus jackpot, the payout for the full house and flush is usually reduced. A 9/6 jacks or better machine will usually be reduced to 8/5 to make up for the progressive jackpot. On a quarter machine, once the progressive for the royal reaches $2,200, the return on the machine becomes positive, making it over 100 percent.

291. Some video poker players work in teams and seek out progressive machines with positive jackpots. They will try to monopolize a whole bank of progressives and play until the jackpot is hit. They then divide the money amongst the team. Many casinos are cracking down to stop the teams.

292. Some casinos run promotions based on certain hands that video poker players are dealt. The casinos will post signs by the bank of video poker machines announcing different promotions. The best way to find out about them is to inquire at the players club before you start playing.

293. The most common promotion is a four-of-a-kind bonus based on the hand of the day: for instance, a bonus if you get four sixes. Some casinos give a scratch card anytime a player gets a four-of-a-kind. It is your responsibility to alert a slot attendant if you are dealt a bonus hand.

294. If you forget to report a bonus to the attendant and hit the draw button by mistake, all may not be lost. You can call the attendant over and they can look at the last five hands that were played. They can confirm that you are entitled to the bonus. If you have played more than five hands, it will be too late.

Bankroll Considerations

295. Risk of Ruin (ROR) is a term that gamblers use to describe the probability of losing your entire starting bankroll before achieving your win goal. In the case of video poker, your win goal is a royal flush. Mathematical simulations have been run to determine the approximate bankroll needed to hit a royal.

296. For a quarter 9/6 jacks or better video poker machine, your chances of hitting a royal before going broke are:

50 percent with a bankroll of $866
75 percent with a bankroll of $1,730
90 percent with a bankroll of $2,880
95 percent with a bankroll of $3,750
99 percent with a bankroll of $5,760
100 percent with an unlimited bankroll

297. On a limited bankroll, the chance of hitting a royal flush on a 9/6 jacks or better machine is 75 percent better than on an 8/5 jacks machine. This is why you always want to pick the machine with the best pay table.

298. The casinos make less on video poker than conventional slots, so some of them reduce the comp given to video poker players. This usually occurs on the machines that offer 100 percent payback. Ask about the casino's policy at the players club when you sign up.

299. Despite reduced comps, video poker is still better than playing slot machines. In most cases, the overall return is much higher. Video poker players enjoy the skill involved in playing the game. If you are only an occasional player, you must approach video poker as you would any other casino game and view it as entertainment.

300. Volatility is word used to describe the "streakiness" of the video poker machine or the fluctuations that will occur with your bankroll. You may have several winning hands in a row and then go through a long period of losing hands. Make sure you have the funds to ride out a losing streak.

301. Don't over-bet your bankroll. If you only have twenty dollars, you should not pick a dollar machine. Remember, it takes five coins for a maximum bet. With twenty dollars, that is four hands playing a dollar machine, sixteen hands playing a quarter machine, and eighty hands playing a nickel machine.

302. Decide ahead of time how long you will play. Before you enter the casino or sit down to play, you should set a time limit and stick to it. Playing longer than four hours will cause fatigue in most players, which can lead to strategy mistakes.

6.

Winning Is Basic: Blackjack

THE BASICS

303. The objective of the game of blackjack is to beat the dealer by having the sum of your card values be higher than the dealer's without going over twenty-one. The goal is to get as close to twenty-one as possible. If you stand (refuse additional cards) and the dealer busts (goes over twenty-one), you win.

304. Anytime your hand or the dealer's hand exceeds twenty-one, it is a bust. This is also referred to as breaking. You will hear these terms used interchangeably; they mean the same thing.

305. The dealer holds the cards in double- and single-deck games. The cards are dealt face down, and the player must pick them up. You are only allowed to pick up the cards with one hand.

306. The device used to hold the cards in a multiple deck game is called a shoe. Cards in a shoe game are dealt face up. You are not allowed to touch your cards.

307. In a shoe game, you must use hand signals when making your playing decisions. You can verbally communicate your decision to the dealer, but you will also be required to make a hand signal. This is done so the "eye in the sky" surveillance cameras can see your actions.

308. Always look at the placard on the table before sitting down. This card shows you the minimum bet for that table.

309. The suits of the cards have no affect on the game. Cards two through ten are counted at face value without regards to their suit. All face cards have a value of ten. An Ace can count as either one or eleven. A Queen and a five would equal fifteen. An Ace and a five would total either six or sixteen.

Playing the Game

310. Blackjack is dealt on a special semi-circle-shaped table that accommodates seven players. There is a separate betting circle or square for each player. The players place their bets in the betting circle in front of their own space. Only chips put in the betting circle count as your bet.

311. You must make your bet before the dealer begins to deal the cards. You will not be allowed to bet once the deal has begun. If you win your bet, the dealer will put your winning chips next to your original bet. Make sure to pick up your winnings before the next deal. Otherwise your winnings will be considered part of you original bet. The saying in the casino is, "If it lays it plays."

312. Never touch, handle, add to, or try to remove your bet once the deal has started. The chips in the circle are considered bets for that play/round and you are not allowed to touch them once the dealer has dealt the first card.

313. If the dealer is dealt an Ace as their "up card," they will offer the players the opportunity to take insurance (see tip 69). After that, they will check the hole card (face down) with the peeking device. If they do not have a blackjack, play will continue. In some casinos, the dealer does not check for a blackjack until after the hand is played out. If the dealer does have a blackjack, everyone loses. The dealer collects all losing bets and the next hand is dealt.

314. When you make an insurance bet you are not really insuring a hand. This is a side bet you make by wagering half your original bet that the dealer has a ten-value card in the hole. If you make the bet and he has the ten, you are paid two to one. You would then lose your original bet but win the insurance bet, which works out to being a push of your original bet. Smart players never take insurance—the casino has a 7 percent edge on this bet.

315. After seeing the first two cards, each player will make his decision. The play proceeds clockwise, starting with the first player to the dealer's left (the player on the right if you are facing the dealer). After seeing your first two cards, you can hit, stand, double down, or split if you have a pair.

316. To take a hit means that you want to draw another card. To signal the dealer for a hit in a shoe game, you will tap the table in front of you or make a beckoning motion with your hand. If you want to take a hit in a hand-held game, you scrape your cards toward you. If you desire another card after the first, you should motion in the same manner. You can keep drawing until you decide to stand or until you bust.

317. If you are satisfied with your cards, you will want to stand. You inform the dealer that you want to stand by waving your hand back and forth over your cards with your palm down. If you want to stand in a hand-held game, you should tuck your cards face down under your bet.

318. When you double down, you double your bet after receiving your first two cards. You then receive only one additional card on your hand. Most casinos will allow you to double down on any two cards. Some casinos limit your doubling to hands that total ten or eleven.

319. To signal that you are doubling down you place an additional bet next to your original bet so you are not adding to or touching your original bet. You can do this as soon as you see your cards. Most casinos will let you double down for less than your original bet providing it meets the table minimum. This is foolish. You only double in favorable situations, and it is to your advantage to double for the maximum and get the most out of the opportunity that you can.

320. If you are dealt a pair with your first two cards, you have the option to split them into two additional hands. If you receive another card of the same value, you can split again. Most casinos will let you split up to four times as long as it is not a pair of aces. For instance, if you are dealt a pair of eights that you split into two hands, and then are dealt another eight, you may "split" that eight into a third hand by making an additional bet.

321. You will play each of your split hands one at a time. The dealer will give you a second card to go with the first split card. You will then decide to hit or stand. After you play out the first hand and stand, you will move on to the next split card and repeat the process.

322. If you are dealt a pair of aces, you are allowed to split them but you only receive one card on each Ace. This is because there is a good chance that your Ace could turn into a twenty-one if you are dealt a ten. If your split aces make twenty-one, you are paid even money. You are not paid the standard three to two odds because the twenty-one was not made with your first two cards. Many casinos will not allow you to re-split aces (that is, split into a third hand if you receive a third Ace after the first pair of aces that you split during that round).

323. To split your cards in a shoe game, you put up an additional bet next to your original bet. Don't separate your cards. The dealer will do it for you. In a hand-held game, you will turn your two cards over and then put up your additional chips for the split. You must bet the same amount as your original wager on the split hand. You do not split your original bet.

324. Rules for blackjack games vary from one casino to the next. Certain rules will favor the player while others will favor the house. It is very important that you check the rules before you sit down to play. You can ask the dealer if you are uncertain about the casino rules or the number of decks being used in the game.

325. The number of decks used makes a difference in the house edge. Normally games using fewer decks are more favorable to the player. When calculating the house advantage for a game, you start with the number of decks used and then add or subtract the edge for the rule variations.

326. Here is the basic casino edge for the number of decks used in a game of blackjack:

Single Deck	Even
Two Decks	0.35 percent
Four Decks	0.52 percent
Six Decks	0.58 percent
Eight Decks	0.61 percent

327. In some casinos, the dealer is required to stand if the total of their cards is seventeen, no matter if the hand contains an Ace (this is denoted in the rules as S17). Other casinos require the dealer to hit seventeen if the hand contains an ace. This is known as a "soft seventeen." (For example, an Ace and a six would be a soft seventeen.) If the dealer hits soft seventeen, the casino gains an edge of 0.20 percent.

328. DOA stands for Double On Any two cards. This is allowed in blackjack games at most casinos. Some casinos have rules restricting your doubling to hands where your first two cards equal nine, ten, or eleven. This rule adds 0.10 percent to the house edge. If you are only allowed to double on ten or eleven, this adds 0.25 percent to the house edge.

329. DAS stands for Double down After Splitting. If you split your cards after being dealt a pair, you will have the option to double when you receive the second card for your split hands. This is a good rule that favors the player. In games where this rule is in effect, the player will gain a 0.13 percent advantage.

330. Late surrender involves giving up your hand in return for half your bet after seeing your first two cards. This can help you to avoid losing everything on a bad hand. It is called late surrender because if the dealer's up card is an Ace, you can only surrender after they have checked for blackjack. The player gains a 0.05 percent advantage for this play.

331. Resplitting aces is a rule variation that is available at some casinos. When you are able to resplit aces, you gain a 0.05 percent advantage. Some casinos let you resplit once while others will let you resplit up to four times.

332. To calculate the house edge, start with the edge determined by the number of decks, then add (for unfavorable rule variations) or subtract (for favorable rules) the edge figures based on the rule variations. For example, a six-deck (0.58 house edge) game where a dealer stands on all seventeens (S17) and doubling after splitting (DAS) (-0.13) is allowed along with late surrender (-0.05), the house edge is 0.40 percent. If you played a six-deck game where the dealer hits soft seventeen (+0.20) and DAS and late surrender was not allowed, the house edge would be 0.78 percent. This particular game has a 0.20 percent higher house edge.

333. Always check the rules before you sit down. If you are visiting a destination that has more than one casino, play at the one offering the best odds. A tenth of a percent may not sound like a big deal, but every little bit helps.

334. Some casinos offer games where blackjack pays six to five instead of three to two. This adds 1.5 percent to the house edge. You should avoid this game. This was done by the casinos to try to win more from the players.

Basic Strategy

335. The house edge in blackjack is derived from the fact that the player must act first. If your hand busts and then the dealer busts, you still lose. Because the casino always wins when the player busts first, they have the advantage.

336. Your two starting cards will fall into one of three categories: hard hands, soft hands, or pairs. A soft hand in blackjack is a hand that contains an Ace. An Ace is worth one or eleven. A hard hand is a hand without an Ace or one for which adding ten would put you over twenty-one.

337. There is a correct mathematical strategy for playing each hand in blackjack. This is called basic strategy, and you should learn it before playing. You will cut the house edge down to less than one percent.

338. Basic strategy is based on the fact that the player gets to see one of the dealer's cards. You are not just blindly trying to draw cards in the dark to get to twenty-one. By seeing one of the dealer's cards you can make an educated guess about the outcome and play your cards accordingly.

Hard Hands

339. A hard hand in blackjack is one that has two starting cards of different values and that does not contain an Ace. The most frequent decision a player will make is whether to stand or hit a hard hand. A hard hand of twelve or more has the potential of busting if you hit it.

340. You have eight and under: With a hard hand of eight or under, you will always hit regardless of the dealer's up card. There is no way you can bust this hand. The only way you can win by standing is if the dealers busts.

341. You have nine: If the dealer's up card is three, four, five, or six, you should double down. Otherwise, you should hit. In a double-deck game, you would double if the dealer showed two through six.

342. There is an easy way to remember the doubling rule for nine in a multi-deck game. You double on three through six, so all you have to do is add them together: three plus six equals nine.

343. You have ten: If the dealer's up card is two through nine, you should double down. Otherwise, hit if the dealer shows a ten or an Ace.

344. You have eleven: If the dealer's up card is two through ten, you should double down. If the dealer shows an Ace, you should hit. In a double-deck game, you would double against a dealer's ace if your eleven was made up of seven and four or six and five.

345. You have twelve: If the dealer's up card is four, five, or six, you should stand. Otherwise, hit. The dealer's chance of busting with four, five, or six is high, so standing is the best play. Hitting when the dealer shows two or three is marginal, but it is the best play.

346. You have thirteen through sixteen: If the dealer's up card is two through six, you should stand. Otherwise, hit. Your hand is terrible, but the dealer is showing a card that can bust if he hits. You are standing in hopes that the dealer will bust.

347. You have seventeen through twenty-one: This is a pat hand. You stand on this hand no matter what the dealer is showing. A seventeen looks like a good hand, but in reality, the average hand to beat the dealer is 19. Note: this rule does not apply for soft hands.

Soft Hands

348. A soft hand in blackjack is a hand that contains an Ace. An Ace is worth one or eleven. If you draw a hand for which eleven would put you over twenty-one, then your hand becomes a hard hand. The Ace is denoted by the letter A in the strategies listed for soft hands. (For example, A-3 means you have one Ace and one three.)

349. You have A-A: This hand actually falls into both the soft hand and pair categories. You should always split this hand. Aces are very powerful and even though you only receive one card on your Ace, it is to your advantage to split this hand.

350. You have A-2 or A-3: If the dealer's up card is four or five, you should double down. Otherwise, hit. The four and five are bust cards for the dealer and you want to take full advantage of the extra money you will make by doubling if the dealer busts.

351. You have A-4 or A-5: If the dealer's up card is four, five, or six, you should double. Otherwise, you should hit. One way to remember this is that when you have a four with the Ace you can double against a four.

352. You have A-6: If the dealer's up card is three, four, five, or six, you should double down. Otherwise, you should hit. This hand is a soft seventeen, but you should never stand with A-6 no matter what the dealer is showing. Doing this is the biggest mistake that novice blackjack players make.

353. You have A-7: If the dealer's up card is three, four, five, or six, you should double down. If the dealer's up card is two, seven, or eight, you stand. If the dealer has a nine, ten, or Ace, you hit. You stand against eight because if the dealer deals himself a ten, you will tie.

354. The A-7 hand is incorrectly played almost as much as the A-6 hand. Players will stand on this hand no matter what the dealer is showing. The average winning hand in blackjack is 19 and standing on soft eighteen against a nine, ten, or Ace will cost the player more money in the long run.

355. You have A-8 or A-9: Always stand no matter what card the dealer is showing. Nineteen and twenty are very powerful hands and you will win more often with this hand. You should never double this hand.

356. You have A-10: Congratulations! You have blackjack and will be paid, providing the dealer does not have blackjack as well. In that case, it would be a push, and you will receive no money. If you are playing a single or double deck game that is dealt face down, you should turn your cards over immediately to show your blackjack.

357. You will double soft hands more often because of the power of the Ace. Too many players fail to take advantage of the opportunities to double down with their soft hands. Don't be afraid of doubling your bet in the correct situations. You will win more in the long run by doubling.

358. A multiple card soft hand is possible and happens frequently after you hit your soft hand. An Ace, two, and three is a soft sixteen and should be played the same as A-5.

Pair Splitting

359. Splitting pairs is either an offensive move or a defensive move depending on the pair and the dealer's up card. You split to win more when the dealer has a bust card showing. You split to lose less when splitting can turn a very bad hand into a potential winner, such as a pair of sevens or eights.

360. If the casino allows you to double down after splitting (DAS), you should take advantage of this whenever possible. You want to get the most money out there when you have the advantage. You will double down on more hands when this rule is in effect.

361. You have a pair of twos or threes: You should split if the dealer's up card is two through seven when DAS is permitted. If you can't double down after splitting, you should only split against the dealer's up cards of four through seven.

362. You have a pair of fours: You should never split a pair of fours. An eight is a much stronger hand than two hands of four.

363. You have a pair of fives: You never split fives because you have ten. You should follow the rules for a hard hand of ten. If the dealer's up card is two through nine, you should double down. Otherwise, hit if the dealer shows a ten or an Ace.

364. You have a pair of sixes: You should split if the dealer's up card is two through seven when DAS is permitted. If you can't double down after splitting, you should only split against the dealer's up cards of three through six.

365. You have a pair of sevens: You should split if the dealer's up card is two through seven. Starting with two hands of seven is better than one hand of fourteen. If you draw a three or a four, you can double down if it is permitted. If you draw a ten, you will have seventeen.

366. You have a pair of eights: You should always split eights. Starting with two hands of eight is better that one hand of sixteen. Splitting a pair of eights is a defensive move. Even against the dealer's up card of ten, you will lose less in the long run.

367. You have a pair of nines: You should split if the dealer's up card is two through six and eight or nine. You stand if the dealer shows a seven because eighteen will beat a seventeen if the dealer's hole card is a ten. You also split nines against a dealer's nine because eighteen is a loser if the dealer has a ten. If you draw ten on your nine, you can tie the dealer.

368. If you have a pair of tens: You should never split. A twenty is a very powerful hand, which will most often win. If you are a card counter, splitting tens when the deck is positive is a sure way to give yourself away.

369. A simple way to learn basic strategy is to use flashcards. Put your hand on the front and the correct strategy decision on the back. For example, on the front of the card you would write "A-7." On the back, you write "Double 3–6. Stand 2, 7, 8. Otherwise hit."

370. If you don't want to memorize basic strategy, you can make or purchase a small card with the strategy printed on it. You are allowed to use the card at the table as long as you do not delay the game.

Side Bets

371. Many casinos offer side bets that can be made in addition to your regular blackjack bet. Some side bets include royal match, six-seven-eight bonus, suited hands, etc. All of these bets should be avoided. You will be dealt fifty to one hundred hands per hour and a dollar side bet on every hand can turn a winning session into a losing one.

Simple Strategy

372. If your first cards total twelve through sixteen, you have a "stiff" hand (one than can be busted with a hit). If the dealer's up card is two through six, it is a stiff hand for the dealer. If you have seventeen or better, it is a pat hand and you stand. If the dealer shows a seven through Ace, you consider it a pat hand. If you have a stiff hand and the dealer has a stiff hand, you stand. If you have a stiff hand and the dealer has a pat hand, you hit.

373. Never stand on a soft hand of seventeen or less. It doesn't matter what the dealer's up card is. Never stand on soft thirteen, fourteen, fifteen, sixteen, or seventeen. You can't bust this hand, so you always have a chance of improving it.

374. Don't try to mimic the dealer's playing strategy by hitting all hands under sixteen and standing on all hands totaling seventeen or more. When you do this, you increase the house advantage to 5.5 percent. There are better strategies for playing your hand.

375. The insurance bet in blackjack is a sucker bet. You are not really insuring anything. This is just an additional bet. Never take insurance unless you are a card counter.

376. In some casinos that offer the surrender rule, you can give up half your bet and not play the hand out. You should surrender hard fifteen against a dealer's ten and sixteen (but not eights) against a dealer's nine, ten, or Ace.

377. Some dealers like to deal the cards at lightning speed. If this makes you uncomfortable, you can slow them down. To do this, just take your time before acting. They cannot go on to the next player until you play your cards. Don't be intimated by fast dealers.

378. The player seated to the far right (to the dealer's left) is referred to as being at "first base." The player to the far left is "third base" or the "anchor player." If you sit at third base, you are the last to act before the dealer.

379. The players at the table usually complain if the player at third base does not play perfect basic strategy. If the player deviates from basic strategy and the dealer wins the hand, the rest of the players at the table will blame the player at third base for their loss. They are wrong because in the long run, the play of others has no affect on the game.

380. Don't give unsolicited advice to other players. They have a right to play the game any way they see fit. They may also be card counters who deviate from basic strategy because of the count.

381. Use a positive progression when you are winning. After you win two hands, increase your bet by one half of your original bet. For example, if you bet ten dollars and win, bet ten dollars again. If you win, go to fifteen dollars. If you win again, go to twenty dollars. Keep progressing until you lose, then go back to your original bet of ten dollars.

382. Lose four, hit the door. If you lose four bets in a row, you should leave the table. Take a break or try a different table. Even if you play perfect basic strategy, you will need a little luck. Changing tables will not change the house edge, but it can help your mental attitude.

383. Avoid playing video blackjack in the slot machines. Most of these games only pay you even money for a natural blackjack. This gives the house a bigger edge. You are better off playing a live game.

384. Card counting is not illegal; however, the casinos do not like players to have the advantage. In Las Vegas and some other casino venues, you can be barred from playing if it is discovered that you are counting cards. In Atlantic City, you cannot be barred, but they can limit the size of your bets.

385. Blackjack players can get an edge over the casino by learning how to count cards. Card counting does not require memorizing cards. You are only keeping track of the mix of cards that are aces or ten in value and the cards lower than ten. This is done by assigning a value to all the plus-ten cards and a value to all the non-ten cards.

386. The simple high-low system assigns a value of minus one to the ten cards and plus one to the non-ten card. You are only required to add or subtract the number one as the cards are dealt.

387. When the deck has more ten-value cards, it is better for the player. This is because a player has a better chance of getting a natural blackjack, which pays three to two. There are also more pat hands as well as a greater chance of the dealer busting if they must draw a card.

388. Card counters gain their advantage by increasing the size of their bets when the deck is rich with ten cards. They reduce their bets when the deck is negative. Many card counters are caught when they raise their bets too much from one hand to the next.

389. Card counting is not difficult, but it does take practice. There are several different counting methods used by the players. Some are simple and some are more complex. There are numerous books and courses to help you learn more about it. Before you attempt card counting, you will have to know how to play perfect basic strategy.

7.

A Dicey Situation: Craps

PLAYING THE GAME

390. Craps is by far the most exciting game in the casino. It is also the most intimidating for new players. Craps is actually an easy game to play and you should give it a try.

391. The craps table is divided into three sections and the game is usually run by four casino employees. The right and left sides of the craps table are identical and this is where the players stand to make their bets. There are two dealers, one for each side, who stand behind the table and are responsible for paying off and collecting bets for their side.

392. A third dealer, called the stickman, stands in front of the table in the center. It is his responsibility to push the dice to the shooter and call out the number that the shooter rolls with the dice. The stickman is in charge of keeping the game running smoothly and placing any proposition bets that are made in the center of the layout.

393. The boxman is the boss of the table and sits in the center behind the table directly opposite the stickman. It is the job of the boxman to watch the dealers to make sure the bets are paid correctly. The boxman settles any disputes that might arise during the game. He or she is responsible for the bank and deposits the money in the drop box when a new player joins the game.

394. To join or buy into a game, you place your money down on the layout and ask for change. Do not try to hand it to the dealer. Do not do this when the shooter has the dice. Wait until the dice are rolled and are in the center of the table between rolls.

395. When you get ready to leave the game, it is best to have all your chips changed to into higher denominations so you won't have to carry a large stack across the casino floor. This is known as coloring up. Wait for the present roll to be completed and ask the dealer to "color up." The dealer will have you place your chips on the table and then give them to the boxman to count.

396. There are about forty different bets that can be made on a craps layout, but most of them (like the proposition and hardway bets) have terrible odds that you should avoid. To get started playing craps, all you need to understand is the basic pass line bet.

397. Basic pass line bet: You place your bet on the pass line before a new shooter begins his roll. This is called the "come out" roll. If the shooter rolls a seven or eleven, you win. If the shooter rolls a two, three, or twelve, you lose.

398. If the shooter rolls any number other than two, three, seven, eleven, or twelve, that number becomes the point number. The shooter must roll that number again before a seven is rolled. If that happens, you win even money for your pass line bet. If a seven is rolled before the point number is rolled again, you lose.

399. The same shooter rolls the dice until they "seven out" (roll a seven) after a point number has been established. If the shooter rolls a two, three, or twelve on the come out roll, they lose their bet, but retain the dice. They just make another pass line bet and roll again.

400. Don't pass bet: This bet is the opposite of the pass line bet. If the shooter rolls a seven or eleven, you lose. If a two or three is rolled, you win. If the twelve is rolled, it is a push. This is known as baring the twelve. The don't pass area is marked on the layout just above the pass line. This is where you place your chips for the don't pass bet.

401. A few casinos offer a game called crapless craps where you still win on a come out roll of seven but the numbers two, three, twelve, and eleven become point numbers which must be repeated before the seven is thrown. Because you no longer win on a natural eleven, this variation of the game increases the house edge on the passline 5.38 percent. You should avoid this game.

402. The reason the don't pass bet ties when the shooter rolls a twelve is because winning this bet would give the player a slight edge over the house. Some casinos bar the two instead of the twelve. The rule will be written on the layout in the area where you make your don't pass bet. There is no difference in the house edge whether the casino bars the two or twelve.

403. You can take down any bet on the craps table except for the pass line bet or the come bet once the point has been established. You can pick up your pass line odds or remove your field bets. You have to ask the dealer to take down your place bets.

404. You can take down your don't pass bet at any time, but you should not do this. During the come out roll, you are at a disadvantage. Once the point is established, the odds shift in your favor.

Odds Bet

405. Because each die has six numbers, thirty-six possible results can be made with a pair of dice. Your odds of rolling a particular number are based on the number of possible ways that number can be rolled. For instance, a three can be rolled two ways: two and one or one and two.

406. Learning the combinations of the dice is not hard because, except for the seven, the other numbers are in pairs. There are six ways to make a seven. There are five ways to make the six and eight, four ways to make the five and nine, three ways to make the four and ten, two ways to make the three and eleven and only one way to make a two or twelve.

407. By knowing the combinations you can quickly determine the true odds of rolling any number. All you have to do is divide thirty-six by the number of possible ways to roll a number. Your odds of rolling a four are thirty-six divided by three (that is, twelve), which means your odds are one in twelve (or as more commonly expressed, eleven to one against you).

408. The pass line bet is an even money bet, so you are paid equal to your pass line bet when you win. It has a house edge of 1.41 percent. You can lower the edge by taking the odds bet behind your pass line bet.

409. Odds bets are paid at true odds, which means you will be paid six to five for the six and eight; three to two for the five and nine; and two to one for the four and ten. If you took ten dollars in odds, you would be paid twelve dollars if the point number was six or eight; fifteen dollars if the point was five or nine, and twenty dollars if the point was four or ten. This is the only bet in the casino that has no house edge. However, in order to make an odds bet, you must first make a pass line bet.

410. The odds bet is the only bet in the game that is not on the craps layout. Once a point is established, players can back their pass line bet with an additional odds bet. You make this bet by placing your bet directly behind your pass line bet on the layout.

411. When you put your odds bet down on the layout, you should adhere to the "two-finger rule." This simply means that there should be a space about two fingers wide between your chip on the pass line and the chips for your odds bet. This is so that a die cannot land and get caught between the two chips. If your odds bet is too close, the dealer may reach over and push it back.

412. Most casinos offer two times odds, which means your odds bet can be twice the amount of your pass line bet. Some casinos offer five, ten, or even one hundred times odds. Higher odds bets lower the casino edge on the pass line bet and are better for the player.

413. The odds bet pays six to five for the numbers six and eight. You must make your odds bets in multiples of five to receive correct payment. If you bet less than five, you will only receive even money for the odd amount. They do not use coins on the craps table, so the lowest denomination is one dollar. The bet pays six dollars for a five-dollar bet. If you bet less than five dollars, you are only paid even money. This means that if you took four dollars in odds, you would only get paid four dollars if you win. However, when you take five dollars in odds, you are paid six dollars.

414. The odds pay three to two for the five and nine. In this scenario, you must make sure that your odds bet is an even amount. The best way to remember this is if the number is odd (five and nine), your odds bet must be even.

415. The odds pay two to one for the numbers four and ten. You will be paid double your odds bet if you win. The odds are higher because it is harder to roll these numbers.

416. Come bets and don't come bets are made after the point is established. They work the same way as the pass and don't pass bets. They are independent of the shooter's point.

417. When a point number is established for a come bet, the dealer will put the bet inside the place box of the corresponding number. You can take odds on your come bet by putting the chips in the come area and telling the dealer you want odds.

418. The odds on the come bet do not work on the new come out roll unless you ask. If the shooter makes his point and then rolls a seven on the come out roll, your come bet will lose, but your odds will be returned to you.

419. When you win a come bet, your original wager and your winnings will be placed in the come area. You must be alert and pick them up before the shooter rolls the dice. If you don't pick it up, it will be considered a bet.

Place Bets

420. To make a place bet, you put your chips in the center of the table and tell the dealer which numbers you want to place. The dealer will then move your chips to the number you want to bet. Place bets are not self-service bets, so don't attempt to do this yourself.

421. The dealer puts your place bet on the layout in a place that corresponds to the location at the table where you are standing. This is how the dealer knows who to pay for the winning bet when there are multiple players placing the same number. When you win a place bet, the dealer will push you your winnings, but the original bet stays up.

422. If you want to take down your place bets, you just tell the dealer to "take me down." If you want to just call off your bet for a roll or two, tell the dealer your bets are off. They will place an off button on your place bets until you wish to continue.

423. A winning place bet on the numbers six and eight pays seven to six odds. You must make your place bets on these numbers in multiples of six dollars. The house edge on the six and eight is only 1.52 percent, which makes it one of the best craps bets in the game.

424. Place bets on the four, five, nine, or ten are made in multiples of five dollars. The four and ten will pay you nine dollars if you win, giving the house a 6.67 percent advantage. The five and nine will pay you seven dollars and have a house edge of 4.76 percent.

Buy and Lay Bets

425. You can buy a number instead of placing it and receive true odds. To do this you must pay a 5 percent commission to the house. Since the minimum chip value at the casino is a dollar, you will be paying at least that much. It is not worth it to buy a number for less than twenty dollars.

426. If you are betting more than ten dollars, buying the four and ten is better than placing them. This is because you are being paid two to one instead of nine to five.

427. Some casinos only charge you the commission on buy bets when you win. Ask the dealer at the table if this is their policy. If you have a choice of casinos to play in, always choose the one that only charges a commission on winning bets.

428. Buying the six and eight is not worth the money. Paying the commission will not be worthwhile. You can place them for less money and you will win more.

429. A lay bet can be made on any of the box numbers. It is the opposite of the buy bet. You will be charged the same commission as you would on the buy bet.

Proposition Bets

430. Proposition bets (or "prop" bets) are long shot bets made at the craps table. Most of the prop bets, except the hardway bets, are one-roll bets. Since you only have one roll of the dice to win or lose, these bets have a very high house edge.

431. Proposition bets are made by tossing your chips to the center of the table to the stickman. Tell the stick person what wagers you want and he or she will put them in the correct place.

432. There are four hardway bets in the center of the craps layouts for the numbers four, six, eight, and ten. When you bet the hardway, you are betting that these numbers will be made by the shooter rolling doubles: two and two for the four, three and three for the six, four and four for the eight, and five and five for the ten. These bets stay up until the shooter rolls the number, sevens out, or makes the number with a combination of the dice that is not a double number (for example, one and three for the four).

433. The "any craps" bet is a one-roll wager that covers the craps numbers two, three, and twelve. If any one of those numbers comes up on the next roll, the player wins. The bet pays seven to one. You can make this bet any time, but most players make it on the come out roll.

434. You can bet on a single craps number. Tell the dealer you want the two, three, or twelve. The twelve is often called midnight. The two and twelve pays thirty to one. The three pays fifteen to one. Like the other prop wages, these are single roll bets.

435. The any seven bet is a wager that the next roll will be a seven. The player loses if any number other than a seven is rolled. The payoff for this bet is only four to one. The house has a 16.70 percent edge on this bet, making it the worst bet on the craps layout.

436. Betting the eleven or "Yo" is a one-roll wager that wins if the shooter rolls eleven on the next roll. It loses if any other number is rolled. The Yo bet pays fifteen to one, but the casino has a huge 11.1 percent house advantage on this bet, so you should avoid it.

437. The C and E bet is a combination of the any craps and the Yo bet. You make this bet in two-dollar increments because you are really making two individual bets. Most players make this bet on the come out roll. There are little circles on the craps layout with the letters C and E where the dealer will place your bets.

438. A horn bet is a one-roll wager on the two, three, eleven, and twelve. It will cost you four dollars because you are actually making a dollar bet on each of the individual numbers. If one of these numbers rolls, you are paid for the winning number minus one dollar for each one of the three losing numbers (three dollars total). For example, if the shooter rolls eleven, you will be paid twelve dollars instead of fifteen ($15 - 3 = 12$).

439. A horn high bet is the same as the horn bet except that the player adds another dollar to one of the numbers covered in the horn bet. The player now bets in multiples of five dollars instead of four dollars and designates which number to wager the additional dollar. A horn high twelve would mean that the player is betting two dollars on the twelve and a single dollar on the two, three, and eleven. This is a one-roll bet as well.

440. A world bet is not noted on the layout, but is a favorite of many players on the come out roll. The wager is made in multiples of five dollars and consists of the four horn numbers (two, three, eleven, and twelve), along with a dollar on the any sevens bet. If the seven is rolled, the wager is a push and the bet stays up for the next roll. You win on the two, three, eleven, and twelve, but lose if any other number is rolled.

441. Hop bets are a one-roll wager on any combination of the two dice. The payout is determined by whether you bet the number as a pair such as five and five or four and four or as a non-pair such as five and one or five and four. A pair will pay thirty to one and a non-pair will pay fifteen to one. Not all casinos allow you to make hop bets.

Etiquette

442. At the craps table you are only allowed to touch the dice with one hand. Make it a habit to pick up the dice with your throwing hand. You cannot switch hands once you pick up the dice.

443. Dice are precision instruments made to strict specification. Rubbing them together can break off the edges. Dice are usually replaced after every eight-hour shift.

444. Dice players are very superstitious. Never say the word seven out loud at the craps table. The other players will give you a dirty look or admonish you for saying it. Seasoned players refer to the seven as "big red" instead of saying the word.

445. When the dice go off the table, many players will call their bets off. Some shooters will request the same die. Before the die is put back in the game, the boxman will inspect it to make sure it has not been switched.

446. The opposite sides (top and bottom) of the dice always add up to seven. One is opposite six, four is opposite three, and five is opposite two. Adjacent sides never add up to seven. A die can be rotated so the one, two, and three appear in view in succession, then turned so the four, five, and six come in rotation. This is a quick way to make sure the dice are legitimate.

447. Never walk up to a table and throw your money in. Take a moment to review the table, the people, and the game in progress. Look to see if the puck is on a number, which will tell you if a point has been established. You don't want to interfere with the shooter.

448. Make your bets while the dice are in the center of the table before the stickman pushes them to the shooter. Once the shooter has the dice, you should keep your hands away from the layout. You don't want the dice to hit your hands.

449. The craps table has rails for you to keep your chips in. Keep your chips directly in front of you and keep your eye on them. Some players have been known to sneak a chip when another player is not looking.

450. When you are the shooter, you are required to hit the back wall with the dice. You do not have to throw them with much force to accomplish this. Don't throw the dice as if you were pitching a baseball.

451. There is a certain camaraderie among dice players. Craps players are very loud and vocal. Don't be afraid to shout or cheer for the point; it's part of the game.

452. Players who make the don't bets tend to be the quiet ones at the table. If you are betting against the shooter, you should not cheer when the shooter sevens out. Since the majority of the players are betting the do side, it is considered bad etiquette to cheer when the others lose.

453. Craps is the fastest moving casino game. Most dealers are efficient, but you should keep track of your bets on the layout to make sure you are paid correctly. When the dealer pays you for a winning bet, it is your responsibility to pick it up from the craps layout.

Terminology and Lingo

454. Betting the do means you are betting the pass line and are rooting for the shooter to make the point. Betting the don't means you are betting the don't pass and want the shooter to seven out.

455. An eleven is called a "Yo" or "Yo-eleven" at the craps table. This is because eleven sounds like seven and it is too easy for players and dealers to confuse.

456. The puck is the marker used to denote the point number. One side is white with the word "on" and the other side is black with the word "off" printed on it. When you see the white "on" in one of the number boxes, it signifies the point.

457. Dealers know where your bets are by how they place your bets on the layout. The bets are placed in the box relative to your position on the rail. Noting where the dealer puts your bet will make it easier for you to watch.

Strategy

458. Make a game plan and stick to it. Don't try to chase the table by switching from pass to don't pass. Switching back and forth will only lead to frustration. If you keep switching from one side to the other, you'll probably find that the other side will come up when you switch.

459. If you want to extend your playing time, stick to the low house edge bets—the pass/don't pass and come/don't come bets, or place the six and eight. These are the best bets you can make. If you do not have a big bankroll, then you should stick to a single pass line bet with odds.

460. An alternative to betting the pass line is to place bets on the six and eight. These numbers have a low house edge. There are five ways to roll a six and five ways to roll an eight, so you actually have ten ways to win. There are only six ways to roll a seven, so the odds of hitting one of these numbers are in your favor.

461. Many players with a larger bankroll will use the three-bet strategy: make a pass line bet, then make two additional come bets with odds taken on all your bets. If your pass line bet wins, you will make another pass line bet. If one of your come bets wins, make an additional come bet so you always have three bets working.

462. Don't load up immediately on every shooter. Start small and progress or spread your bets to take advantage of a hot shooter. This will minimize your losses if there is a quick seven out. Make sure to get your original money back before you start increasing your bets.

463. Decide how much money you are willing to risk in one session. Then find a table that offers the limits to fit your bankroll. You should have a bankroll equal to at least fifty times your bet. Being under-capitalized will increase your risk of going broke if you hit a few cold shooters.

464. Some craps layouts have a "Big 6/8" betting area. You put your bet in this area and if a six or eight is rolled, you are paid even money. This is a bad bet and you should never make it. It is to your advantage to place the six and eight.

465. A hedge bet involves making two offsetting bets, one of which pays off slightly more than the other. Hedging a bet means taking a second bet on the table that will win if the first bet looses. This way, if one bet loses, then the other wins and you haven't lost your money and you may make a very small profit.

466. Some players like to hedge their bets by placing the point number while they have a bet on the don't pass line. For example, you bet ten dollars on the don't pass line and the shooter rolls a six, which becomes the point number. You make a place bet on the six for six dollars. If the shooter sevens out, you collect ten dollars for the don't pass bet and lose six dollars for the place bet, giving you a four dollar profit. If the shooter makes his point by rolling a six, you lose your ten dollar don't bet, but collect seven dollars for your place bet for a three dollar loss.

467. A craps check is a term used by players when they make the "any craps" bet during the come out roll. This bet is a hedge bet that players make to try and protect their pass line bet if the shooter throws a craps number. This is not a smart bet to make as the high house edge makes it a losing proposition over the long run.

468. Some craps players use the patience system. They will wait until a shooter has made three points in a row, and then bet against the shooter. The probability of a shooter making three points in a row is one in eight.

Dice Setting

469. Controlled shooting is a term used for shooting the dice the same way each time. Some players also call it rhythm rolling. Lately, more players have acknowledged that there is some validity in rhythm rolling. There are hundreds of shooters who practice throwing the dice at home on private craps tables or special practice boxes to increase the odds of rolling certain numbers and not rolling a seven after the point is established.

470. The concept behind rhythm rolling is to start by setting the dice in a certain manner, gripping them and throwing them the same way each time. This produces a "controlled throw." The desired result is to alter the random outcome of the two dice when they land, producing a particular desired result with greater frequency than random throwing will generate.

471. Most craps players have witnessed a hot roll in which the shooter threw number after number before he sevened out. By throwing the dice in the same manner each time, some shooters get into a rhythm that has produced monstrous rolls. Some shooters who try to practice rhythm rolling do this consciously, while others are unaware that they are doing it.

472. The first step in controlled shooting is setting the dice. The shooter wants to start with the dice facing the same way. The most common dice set is the hardway set. Controlled shooters have found this set helps avoid the seven after the point is established.

473. To set the dice for the hardway set, you have one of the hard numbers on all the facing dice. Have the same number facing up and the same front number each time. The hard numbers are:

Hard ten made with the dice five and five
Hard eight with dice four and four
Hard six with the dice three and three
Hard four with the dice two and two

474. An example of the hardway set would be to have the five and five on top. The four and four sides of the dice would be in the back facing you and the three and three in front. This would mean the two and two are on the bottom.

475. It takes practice to set the dice quickly. If you persist in holding up the game, a dealer can legally take the dice away from you and pass them to the next shooter. This isn't done too often, as it tends to make the other players mad, but it can happen.

476. After setting the dice, you need to throw them with a 45-degree arch down the table. Your throw must be soft as you want to land them so they just touch the back of the table. You don't want to throw them with a lot of force because the more they bounce, the more random your throw becomes.

477. There are books on the market and websites on the Internet devoted to dice setting, rhythm rolling, and dice control. GoldenTouchCraps.com offers courses in dice control.

478. If you have no desire to learn how to set the dice, look for a shooter who is setting the dice and taking care in the way they shoot. They won't have a big roll each time, but many of them will have longer rolls than the shooter who whips the dice down the table. Not all dice setters are controlled shooters, but their efforts show that they are taking the game seriously and trying to win.

8.

Go for a Spin: Roulette

THE BASICS

479. Roulette is the oldest table game in the casino. It originated in France, and the modern layout we use today was developed around 1842. Roulette dealers are sometime referred to as croupiers. The French word for dealer is croupier.

480. The object of roulette is to pick the winning number where the ball will land on the spinning roulette wheel. You can also bet combinations of numbers, choose the color, or whether it is odd or even. It is not as easy as it seems.

481. Dealers are required to keep the wheel moving at all times, even between spins. They spin the ball in the opposite direction of the wheel's spin. This causes the ball to jump and spin before landing on a number.

482. Many casinos use two different-sized balls at the roulette table. Some dealers prefer one to the other, depending on the size of their hand. A player may request a change although this is not too common.

483. The numbers zero, double zero, and one through thirty-six are placed on the wheel so number one is opposite number two, three is opposite four, etc. A red number is next to a black number, and there are no more than two even numbers in a row. The zero and double zero are green and are opposite each other on the wheel.

484. All the numbers on the roulette wheel add up to 666. Two adjacent numbers of the same color add up to thirty-seven most of the time. A perfect arrangement is not possible because the even numbers add up to 342 and the odd numbers add up to 324.

485. Roulette's layout has two betting areas. The inside betting area contains the individual numbers on the layout. The outside betting area has boxes with columns for red/black, odd/even, and different groups of numbers.

486. The inside betting area has boxes for the numbers one through thirty-six, arranged in a grid that is three numbers wide by twelve numbers tall. American roulette wheels also have a zero and a double zero. European roulette wheels only have a single zero. You can find a single-zero wheel in some American casinos as well, although they are not common.

487. Inside bets in roulette are wagers made on specific numbers or combinations of the numbers on the layout. Outside bets are wagers made in the boxes in the outer area of the layout that include the red, black, odd, even, or groups of numbers.

488. A straight-up bet is a wager on a single number. The casino pays thirty-five to one when you win. This is the most difficult bet to hit, but the biggest payout in the game.

489. A split bet is a wager on two numbers, and it pays seventeen to one. You make this bet by placing your chip so it straddles the line between any two numbers. Splits can be made from any two adjacent numbers.

490. A street bet is also called a line bet, and it pays eleven to one. This is a wager of three numbers in a horizontal row. You make this bet by placing your chip on the vertical line separating the outside and inside betting areas. The chip straddles the first number in the row.

491. A corner bet, or quad bet, pays eight to one. You make this bet by placing a chip on the intersection of a vertical and horizontal line inside the layout. Your chip will be touching one corner of each of the four numbers you are betting.

492. The basket bet is a five number bet on zero, double zero, one, two, and three. It pays six to one. On the double-zero wheel, this bet has a house edge of 7.89 percent, making it the worst bet in roulette. You should avoid making the basket bet.

493. The double street bet is a wager on six numbers and pays five to one. You place your chip on the line separating the outside and inside area as you do for the street bet, but place it so that it also straddles the row above or below. You now have the six numbers from two rows.

Outside Bets

494. Red or black bets are even money bets made by placing your wager in either of the corresponding boxes on the outside layout. There are eighteen red numbers and eighteen black numbers. The zero and double zero are green, and you lose your red and black bets on the American wheel if one of them rolls.

495. Odd or even bets also pay even money when you win. You place your wager in a numbered box on the layout. There are eighteen odd and eighteen even numbers. The zeros are neither odd nor even, and you lose if they are rolled.

496. A low bet is made by placing your wager in the box marked one through eighteen. A high bet is made by placing your wager in the nineteen through thirty-six box. These are even money bets, which lose if the zero or double zero is rolled.

497. En prison is an option offered in some games where you get a second chance if the zeros come up when you make an even money bet. Your bet is held for one more spin and if you win on the next spin, you get your original bet back.

498. Surrender is a modified version of en prison offered by some American casinos. On even money bets, you only lose half your wager if the zeros are rolled. You can leave your money on the layout and go for a push or take back the half bet.

499. Dozens bets are made on twelve consecutive numbers. You place your wager in the boxes marked one through twelve, thirteen through twenty-four, or twenty-five through thirty-six. These bets pay two to one. If the zero or double zero comes up, you lose.

500. Column bets are also twelve-number bets. Instead of twelve consecutive numbers, they consist of the numbers in one of the three vertical columns and are made in the boxes at the bottom of the layout. These bets pay two to one as well.

501. Many casinos allow players at the far end of the table to split the zeros by placing a bet on the courtesy line, which is the line separating the second and third dozens boxes. This is the only inside bet made in the outside area.

General Tips

502. Since there are thirty-eight numbers total, including the zero and double zero, the house edge on the American wheel is 5.26 percent. The single zero European wheel has a house edge of 2.63 percent and is a better game for the player.

503. Roulette is one of the slower games in the casino. Although roulette has a high house edge, you will only get about thirty decisions per hour. This reduces the amount of time your money is at risk.

504. Try to play at a full roulette table rather than one with only a few players. This will slow the game down, decreasing your exposure to the house edge. It will also increase your comp time.

505. All casinos have minimum and maximum betting limits on their table games. The table minimums for inside and outside bets are the same. However, because of the higher payouts on inside bets, the maximum betting limits for the inside bets are usually lower than those for the outside bets.

506. You can't combine your inside and outside bets to meet the table minimum. If the minimum bet is five dollars, you have to bet five dollars on the inside and/or five dollars on the outside. You can't bet three dollars inside and two dollars outside.

507. If you are playing the inside on a five dollar table you can split your bets into five separate one dollar bets. You could play five numbers straight up or combine any of the other inside bets as long as all your bets total the table minimum. If you want to play the outside bets you can split those up as well amongst any of the different outside bets.

508. Each roulette player at the table has his own color chips. This helps the dealer determine who to pay. The player must cash in these chips when he leaves the roulette table.

509. The casino wants to avoid disputes. Since each player has his own color chips, you are not allowed to share your chips with another player. If you are playing with a friend who runs out of chips, he will have to purchase more of his own color.

510. When you buy in, tell the dealer what denomination chips you want. He or she will put a small circular marker next to the wheel that tells how much your chips are worth. When you cash out, the dealer will pay you in standard casino chips.

511. A player making a quick bet on the outside numbers may be allowed to play with regular casino chips. If more than one player is doing this, you must watch your bet carefully to make sure your winnings are not picked up by another player.

512. If you like to play the inside numbers, you should take a seat on the side, in the middle of the table. This will make it easier to reach all the numbers on the layout.

513. Since it is difficult to reach the numbers at the top of the layout if you are sitting at the end of the table, you can tell the dealer what numbers you want to bet and he will place the chips for you. This way you avoid leaning over the table.

514. If the number you want to bet is already covered with chips, don't worry. It is permissible to stack your chips on top of the other chips. This is another reason why each player has his own color chips.

515. The dealer marks the winning number with a marker. You are not allowed to place your bet for the next spin until the dealer removes the marker from the previous winning number. Make sure you wait for them to pick it up before putting down your chips.

516. When you win a bet on the inside numbers, the dealer will add up all your winning bets and push your chips to you. Your original bet will stay on the layout. If you don't want to repeat the bet, you have to remove it on your own.

517. The dealer will pay the outside bets first by placing the winnings next to the original bet. You are not allowed to pick these up until the inside bets are paid and the marker is removed from the layout.

518. You are allowed to place bets after the dealer spins the ball. The dealer will tell you when to stop. As the ball slows down, the dealer will wave their hand over the table and call out "No more bets."

519. Everybody seems to think they have a surefire system for winning at roulette. The truth is there is no system that will change the house edge. Don't waste your money buying a roulette system.

520. Bet with the trend. If red has been coming up, bet red. Don't assume that black is "due." Many players bet against the trend.

521. On July 14, 2000, at Caesars Palace in Las Vegas, the number seven came up six times in a row. The odds of this happening are about three billion to one.

522. A roulette table accommodates about eight players. Since space is at a premium, spectators are not allowed to sit down and watch. Someone who is not playing should stand behind the players with bets on the table.

523. You can win multiple bets on the same number by using it in different inside bets. Bet a number straight up and combine it with a split, corner, street, or double street bet. You not only win more if it hits, but you hedge your bet if a different number you have covered comes in.

524. A sector or zone is a group of numbers that are adjacent to each other on the wheel. Using a picture of the wheel will help you determine if a certain sector is being hit. Players like to place their bets in the hot sector.

525. Some dealer's actions become so mechanical they spin the ball the same way every time. When this happens, the ball tends to land in the same sector. This is known as a dealer's signature and if you detect it, you can place your bets in the sector that is being hit.

526. Many players chart the numbers to determine a dealer signature or a biased wheel. This is known as "clocking" the wheel; some teams will spend twenty-four consecutive hours recording spins.

527. A neighbor bet is a wager on a number, the two numbers on the left of it on the wheel, and the two numbers on the right. This gives you a sector bet of five numbers. You don't have to know the numbers. Tell the dealer your primary number and say your want a neighbor bet.

528. Roulette wheels are precision instruments. They must be perfectly balanced to insure a random spin. The walls between the numbers are called frets. If the frets are worn or the wheel is not balanced, it can cause a biased wheel.

529. Most casinos now have electronic display boards that show the last twenty numbers spun on the wheel. This makes it easier to keep track of the numbers than writing them by hand.

Strategy

530. Use a positive progression when you are winning. Increase your bets only if you win. Never double up if you lose. This is a Martingale and is discussed in the Money Management section in Chapter 3.

531. If you are betting one chip on five numbers straight up and one of them hits, you will have a profit of thirty chips. Increase each of the five numbers by one chip. If you win again, increase the bet to three chips. If you lose the next spin, go back to one chip on each number.

532. The quad strategy consists of making five quad bets. You are covering twenty numbers with five chips. If one of your bets hits, you will be paid eight chips. Re-bet the losing quads and increase the winning quad by one chip and you will have a three-chip profit if your bet hits again.

533. My favorite strategy is to bet two chips on the ten/thirteen and twenty-eight/thirty-one double streets and one chip on the seventeen, eighteen, twenty, twenty-one quad. You have sixteen numbers covered that are spread around the wheel. If one of the bets wins, increase it by one chip on the next spin.

534. Place one chip on black, which will cover the eighteen black numbers and make a one-chip column bet on the third column (under the thirty-six), which has nine red numbers. If you prefer, you can bet red and make a column bet on the second column, which has nine black numbers. Many times, you will break even, but occasionally you win will three chips.

535. The split strategy involves making nine split bets that will cover eighteen numbers. Place bets splitting; 1-4, 5-8, 9-12, 14-17, 16-19, 20-23, 24-27, 29-32, and 31-34. If one of your numbers hits, you will be paid seventeen, giving you a nine-chip profit. You can pick your own numbers, but be sure to spread them around the layout.

536. Bet one chip on a double street and make four straight up bets. You will have ten numbers covered. If the double street wins, you make a one-chip profit. If your straight up bet wins you will make a thirty-one-chip profit. Play the same numbers for four spins.

537. When you parlay a bet, you let the winnings ride along with the original bet. If you parlay a straight up roulette bet, you will be betting thirty-six chips on the second spin. (This is your original bet of one chip and your thirty-five winning chips.) It will pay 1,260 if the number hits twice in a row.

538. If you see someone hitting big, follow their lead and play the bets they are making. It might be his lucky day and you can ride his coattails. It may not help, but it might be better than picking your own numbers.

539. Miss four, hit the door. If you don't hit a number in four spins, move to another table or take a break for a while. Luck is not with you and you don't want to play too long at a losing table.

9.

Is This Seat Taken?: Other Table Games

Baccarat

THE BASICS

540. Baccarat is a game that many new players mispronounce by calling it "back-er-rat." The "t" is silent, and it is correctly pronounced "baa-ca-rah." Learn to pronounce it correctly if you don't want to sound like a novice.

541. Baccarat is one of the best games you can play. The house edge is low, offering the player an almost even game. There are no strategy decisions that will change the house edge.

542. The house edge for a bet on the banker is 1.06 percent. The house edge on the player bet is 1.24 percent. The house edge is 14.36 percent if you bet on the tie. In order to make it more even, a 5 percent commission is collected for a winning banker bet.

543. There is a mystique surrounding the game of baccarat that makes it intimidating to the average player. Many players don't even give the game a second look because they think it is highly sophisticated or complicated. The truth is that it is about as difficult as picking a coin toss.

544. Baccarat is played in a pit on a large table that can accommodate twelve to fourteen players. Each seat is numbered; however, there is no seat number thirteen on the layout. Some casinos enforce a strict dress code for the players in the baccarat pit.

545. The cards are dealt out of a shoe, which contains eight decks of cards. In baccarat, the shoe is called the bank. The bank is passed around the table and each player will take a turn dealing the cards.

546. Regardless of the number of players at the table, only two hands are dealt, one for the player and one for the banker. A player can bet on either hand except when they are dealing the cards, at which time they can only bet the banker.

547. Three dealers are present at the baccarat table. One dealer, known as the "caller," runs the game. The caller stands by the table and announces the point totals of the cards as they are dealt by the banker.

548. The two additional dealers are seated at the table on each side of the caller. It is their responsibility to pay off winning bets and collect losing bets. The dealers also keep track of the commission that is paid on a banker's bet.

549. Players wagering on the banker must pay a 5 percent commission when they win. There are numbered squares on the layout corresponding to the player's seat number in front of the dealers. The dealers keep track of the commissions owed by the players. These are paid at the end of each shoe or when a player leaves the table.

550. Many high rollers play baccarat and quite often you hear about wins or losses exceeding a million dollars or more. The house edge is low for this game and a player catching a winning streak can rack up some large wins.

551. The minimum bet in the baccarat pit is much higher than games out on the casino floor. It is not uncommon to see table minimums of fifty or one hundred dollars. The higher table limits keep most average players away from the game.

552. Around 1980 the casinos introduced mini-baccarat to make the came more accessible to the average player. Mini-baccarat is played on the casino floor at a blackjack style table. The dealer handles all the cards.

553. The betting limits are much lower for mini-baccarat. Since there are fewer players at the table, the game is played much faster. The rules for the game are the same as the larger version.

How to Play Baccarat

554. The object of the game is to bet on the hand with a sum that comes closest to nine. Occasionally the two hands will tie, but betting on a tie gives up too much of a house edge to be profitable.

555. Each hand begins with the players making a bet. A player can only make three choices in the game of baccarat. They can bet on the player, the banker, or a tie. All decisions for drawing cards are set in the rules. There are betting squares on the layout in front of each seat. Players put their bets in the appropriate box (player, banker, or tie), and the deal begins.

556. The banker acts as the dealer and slides one card out of the shoe. He passes it face down to the "caller," who passes it to the player with the largest bet. Another card is dealt for the banker's hand and is placed next to the shoe. A second card is dealt to the player and then a second card is dealt for the banker's hand.

557. The player turns over his or her hand first. In the baccarat pit, the player will usually make quite a ceremony of doing this. You will see players crimp and bend the cards and slowly roll them over to expose the total.

558. The casinos allow this time-consuming ritual for the benefit of the large bettors. The amount of money wagered makes up for the delay in the game. At a mini-baccarat table, the dealer turns over both hands and the play is completed much faster.

559. If you are the player, you should not look at your hand until both hands are dealt. If you are the banker, you should not look at your cards until the player has finished turning over his hand. This standard etiquette is adhered to during the game.

560. The numeric value of the cards in baccarat is the only thing considered; the suit of the card is meaningless. The numbers two through nine are counted at face value. An Ace counts as one. Tens, jacks, queens, and kings are counted as zero. Ten is subtracted from hands that total more than nine.

561. The easiest way to remember the score is to drop the first digit of the total. A total of thirteen becomes three, sixteen becomes six, and two face cards that total twenty would become zero.

562. The highest possible hand is a nine. A total of eight or nine with the first two cards is called a natural. If the player receives a natural, it is an automatic winner unless the dealer ties it or has a nine to beat the eight.

563. After the player's first two cards are turned over, the banker will turn over his cards. If neither player has a natural, then play will continue based on the predefined rules of the game. The player will draw or stand depending on the total of her hand and the banker will draw or stand based on the player's hand.

564. If a player's first two cards total six or seven, she is required to stand. If the total of the player's two cards are zero through five, then the player must draw a third card. If the banker has a natural, the hand is over, and the banker wins.

565. If the player stands on two cards totaling six or seven, the banker must draw if his cards are zero though five. The banker must stand if his cards totals six or more. If both the player and banker have hands that require them to stand on, the one with the highest total wins.

566. If the player draws a third card, the banker must draw or stand depending on the value of the player's third card. This is where the rules get confusing for some players; however, these rules do not have to be memorized because the caller will instruct the banker to draw or stand.

567. The banker's first two cards total zero, one, or two: The banker will always draw. The banker's first two cards total seven: The banker will always stand. It does not matter what the player's third card is.

568. The banker's first two cards total three: The banker must draw if the player's third card is zero through seven. The banker will stand if the player's third card is eight.

569. The banker's first two cards total four: The banker must draw if the player's third card is two through seven. The banker stands if the player's third card is zero, one, eight, or nine.

570. The banker's first two cards total five: The banker must draw if the player's third card is four through seven. The banker stands if the player's third card is zero, one, two, three, eight, or nine.

571. The banker's first two cards total six: The banker must draw if the player's third card is six or seven. The banker stands if the player's third card is anything else.

BACCARAT STRATEGY

572. Remember that you must settle and pay your commissions for betting the banker's hand before you leave the table. Make sure you have enough money left to do this. Don't bet your last chips unless your commission is paid.

573. Never bet the tie. The high house edge makes this one of the worst bets in the casino. Stick to betting on the banker or the player.

574. There is no strategy for baccarat that will change the outcome of the game. Many players like to track the outcome and look for trends. The casino supplies sheets you can use to do this.

575. You are not required to bet every hand. If you want to sit out for a hand or two, you may do so. Many players do this if they are betting a trend.

576. The banker hand will win more frequently than the player hand. If you are going to bet a trend, it is better to bet the banker trend. Bet on the banker hand until it looses, then wait until the player hand loses, and start betting banker again.

577. Use a positive progression when you are winning. Bet the same amount until you have two wins in a row. After winning two bets in a row, increase your bet by one half unit. If you are betting fifty dollars a hand, the progression would be: fifty, fifty, seventy-five, seventy-five, one hundred, one hundred, etc. Go back to your original bet after a loss.

578. Avoid the Martingale betting system. Don't double up after a loss. Make sure you set a stop loss before you begin playing.

Let It Ride

THE BASICS

579. Shuffle Master, a company that manufactures machines to shuffle cards, invented let it ride in 1993. Shuffle Master owns the rights to the game and any casino that wants to have it on the casino floor must use the Shuffle Master machine.

580. Let it ride quickly became one of the most popular table games in the casino. Part of the appeal is due to the fact that the player can take back a portion of their original bet during the game. If the player has a good hand, she can "let it ride" and collect the win for her full bet, hence the name of the game. The game is also popular because it offers a potential for high payouts.

581. Let it ride is based on five-card stud poker. It uses two community cards that players share with their own three personal cards to form a five card hand. Payoffs are made based on a pay table similar to that of video poker.

582. The hand rankings are the same as in poker and video poker. The object of the game is to get a pair of tens or better. You are not playing against the other players and the dealer does not play. Because the players are not playing against each other or trying to beat the dealer, camaraderie develops amongst the players, creating a fun atmosphere.

583. Let it ride can also be a good game for the recreational player because it is exciting, but slower than blackjack. You will be dealt about forty hands per hour. Some casinos offer lower limit games. If you take the time to learn the simple strategy, you can enjoy this table game and reduce the house edge to 3.5 percent.

How to Play Let It Ride

584. The game is played on a table similar to a blackjack table. There are three circles in front of each player on the table. The circles are marked "1," "2," and "$." To start the game, a player places three equal bets, one bet in each circle.

585. The Shuffle Master machine deals out cards three at a time. The dealer places a three-card hand in front of each player and one three-card hand in the center of the table. After each player receives his cards, the dealer discards one card from the three-card hand at the center of the table, leaving two cards face down in front of the dealer.

586. The machine counts out the remaining cards into the discard tray. When this is finished, the players are allowed to look at their three-card hand. You are not supposed to touch your cards until the machine finishes counting the discards.

587. After the machine accounts for the cards, the players are allowed to look at their three-card hand. At this point, you have the option to take back your bet in circle number one or let it ride. The dealer will work clockwise asking each player in turn to make a decision.

588. To take back your bet, you scrape your cards on the table toward you or make a brushing motion with your hand. The dealer will push your bet back to you. You are not allowed to remove the chips on your own.

589. If you like your hand after seeing your first three cards, you can leave all your bets up. To do this, you place your cards face down under your chips. This signals to the dealer that you want to let bet number one ride.

590. After all the players have made their decisions, the dealer will turn up the first of the two community cards that are in front of the dealer. This card is used as the fourth card for all the players' hands. You now have the option of taking down your second bet or letting it ride.

591. You are permitted to take down your second bet even if you let your first bet ride. Tell the dealer you want your second bet down and then put your three cards under the chip in the $ circle. You cannot take down the first bet or put it back up.

592. After seeing the first community card and making your decision on the second bet, your decisions are over. Your third bet must remain up. You do not have the option of taking it down.

593. After all the players make their decisions for the second bet, the dealer will turn up the second community card. This card completes the five-card hand for every player. At this point, the dealer will pay all the winning bets according to the pay table.

594.

The pay table looks like this:

Royal Flush	1,000 to 1
Straight Flush	200 to 1
Four-of-a-Kind	50 to 1
Full House	11 to 1
Flush	8 to 1
Straight	5 to 1
Three-of-a-Kind	3 to 1
Two Pairs	2 to 1
Pair of Tens or Better	1 to 1

595.

If you have a winning hand, you will be paid for all the bets you let ride. For example, if you bet one chip in each circle and left all three bets up, you would be paid twenty-four chips for a flush. If you took back the first bet, you would only be paid sixteen for the remaining two bets that you let ride.

LET IT RIDE STRATEGY

596.

The house edge for the basic game is approximately 3.5 percent when you play the correct strategy. You must know which hands you should take down and when to let it ride. If you play on hunches, the house edge will be considerably greater. The following tips describe the proper strategy for this game.

597. Let bet number one ride if you have...

- A winning hand (a pair of tens or better)
- A three-card royal flush
- A three-card straight flush

598. Let bet number two ride if you have...

- A winning hand (a pair of tens or better)
- A four-card royal or straight flush
- A four-card flush
- Four high cards
- A four-card, open-ended straight

599. If your first three cards are terrible, all is not lost. There is a possibility that the two community cards will be a pair of tens or higher. This will happen about once in forty hands, so you would still take down your first two bets.

600. Be aware that you will only win about 25 percent of your hands. Make sure you have a big enough bankroll to handle the losing streaks you will surely encounter in this game.

Let It Ride Side Bets

601. There is an additional side bet you can make for a dollar when playing let it ride. This bet pays a bonus for certain hands, usually a straight or higher. The pay tables for the bonus hands vary from casino to casino. The house edge ranges from 15 to 30 percent on these bets. As with most side bets offered by the casino, this bet should be avoided.

602. In 1995, Shuffle Master created a tournament. Every three to six months, players who got a royal flush when they made the side bet were invited to an exclusive let it ride tournament. The winner of the tournament received one million dollars. Unfortunately, the tournament has been discontinued.

Let It Ride Etiquette

603. Players must act in turn. Since the dealer is required to push your bet back to you, it will do you no good to scratch at the table until the dealer gets to you. If you are letting your bet ride, you can tuck your cards under your bet ahead of time.

604. Players should make their decisions quickly when it is their turn to act. Don't be dramatic by squeezing your hand or peaking under the edge. It is best to look at your cards and make your decision before it is your turn to act.

605. Players are not permitted to show each other their hands even though you are not playing against each other. Having knowledge of the card in someone else's hand can affect your strategy decisions. If you do show your cards, you will be admonished by the dealer.

606. At the end of the hand, the dealer will turn your cards over and check for a winning hand. Don't touch your cards once you have made your final decisions by placing them under the chip in the final $ circle.

607. If you want to tip the dealer by making a bet for them, it must go in the third circle marked with the dollar sign. You are not allowed to pull back this bet. In let it ride, it is better just to give your tip directly to the dealer.

Caribbean Stud

THE BASICS

608. Caribbean stud originated in the Caribbean Islands. In the 1980s, it was introduced on cruise ships and became very popular, slowly making its way to the casinos in the early nineties.

609. The game is based on five-card stud poker; the ranking of hands are the same as other poker games. You are playing against the dealer, and your hand must beat the dealer's hand. You do not have to worry about beating the other players' hands.

610. Caribbean stud is played on a blackjack-sized table that accommodates up to seven players. In front of each player are areas marked "ante" and "bet." There is also a slot to place a chip for the additional side bet.

CARIBBEAN STUD PLAY

611. The game starts with each player making an ante bet equal to the table minimum. This is placed in the circle marked ante in front of the player. At this time, the player also has the option of making an additional dollar side bet for the bonus jackpot.

612. An automatic shuffler deals the cards, and the dealer hands each player their cards in turn. Each player receives a hand with five cards face down. You can look at your cards by picking them up with one hand. The dealer's hand has four cards down and one card up.

613. The players look at their cards and make a decision to fold and forfeit their ante bet or call by making an additional bet twice the size of the ante. If you are playing at a five-dollar table, your ante bet would be five dollars and your call bet would be ten dollars.

614. After all the players have bet or folded, the dealer's four remaining cards are turned face up. The dealer must qualify by having a hand with an Ace and King or a higher poker hand such as a pair or better for play to continue. If the dealer does not qualify, the players are paid even money for their original ante bet and the second call bet is a push, which means it does not win or lose.

615. If the dealer does qualify and your hand beats the dealer, you will be paid even money for your ante bet and your call bet will be paid according to the following pay table.

One Pair or Less	1 to 1
Two Pairs	2 to 1
Three-of-a-Kind	3 to 1
Straight	4 to 1
Flush	5 to 1
Full house	7 to 1
Four-of-a-Kind	20 to 1
Straight Flush	50 to 1
Royal flush	100 to 1

616. The house edge for the basic game is over 5.2 percent because of the instances in which you lose the original bet. However, with the call bet factored in, the element of risk (the ratio of money lost to total money wagered) is about 2.55 percent.

617. This game is slower paced than blackjack, and it is more of a social game like let it ride. Because of the slower pace, the house edge won't hurt your bankroll too much if you play for smaller stakes. Keep in mind that you must also avoid making the side bet.

CARIBBEAN STUD SIDE BETS

618. Caribbean stud offers an additional dollar side bet that gives the player a chance to win the bonus jackpot. In order to win the side pot, you must have a flush or better.

619. A percentage of every dollar wagered on the side bet is added to the progressive jackpot. This varies in different casino jurisdictions, but it is usually no more than 70 percent. The average house edge on the side bet is over 26 percent.

620. You need a flush or higher to qualify for one of the bonus payouts, and the money you win when you receive one of these hands is not close to the odds of doing so. You will make a flush once every 508 hands and for this the casino will pay you fifty dollars.

621. You are paid a fixed amount for each qualifying hand. A flush is paid fifty to one. The odds are 508 to 1. A full house is paid seventy-five to one. The odds are 693 to 1. A four-of-a-kind is paid one hundred to one. The odds are 4,164 to 1.

622. If you are dealt a straight flush, you will receive 10 percent of the progressive jackpot. If you are dealt a royal flush, you will receive the entire progressive jackpot. Once the royal is hit, the progressive meter is usually reset at fifty thousand dollars.

623. The odds of being dealt a royal flush in stud poker are 649,740 to 1. Even with the other bonus payouts factored into the jackpot, it is not a worthwhile bet. The progressive meter would have to be around $236,300 to justify making the side bet.

624. If you choose to make the side bet, you are eligible for the jackpot even if the dealer does not qualify. You must inform the dealer immediately before he or she picks up the cards. Normally the dealer will pick up all the cards without turning them over.

CARIBBEAN STUD STRATEGY

625. The player must act before the dealer. There will be many times that you fold and the dealer does not qualify with ace-king or better, but this does not mean you should play every hand. The dealer will qualify about 82 percent of the time.

626. The strategy for Caribbean stud is very simple to learn. Call if you have an Ace-King or better. Fold any other hand. Avoid the side jackpot.

627. Many players like the slow pace and relaxed atmosphere of Caribbean stud. There are a lot of games offering a lower house edge that you can play in the casino. If you must play, stick to the basic game and avoid the side bets.

THE BASICS

628. Pai gow is pronounced "pie gow." It is a Chinese game played with dominos called tiles. The American version uses cards instead of tiles and is actually pai gow poker; however, most players refer to the game simply as pai gow.

629. Pai gow is played with a fifty-two-card deck and one joker. The joker can be used as an Ace or it can be used as a wild card for completing a straight, flush, or straight flush only. It is played on a blackjack-style table that can seat up to seven players.

630. The game is very slow paced. The players compete one on one against the banker/dealer, and not against each other. There are quite a few ties, which means under most circumstances, your bankroll will last quite a while.

631. The odds are fairly even between the player and the dealer. The dealer has a slight advantage because he wins a tie if both hands are exactly the same. The player must pay a 5 percent commission on a winning hand.

632. Players may opt to act as the banker/dealer. To do this you must have enough money to cover all the bets made by the other players. The banker is required to pay the house a commission on all the hands he wins.

633. The deal rotates around the table. If a player does not want to be the banker, then the casino dealer will handle the duties. The deal is rotated so that one player cannot monopolize the deal. Some casinos will let you deal more than one hand, but there is usually a limit.

How to Play Pai Gow

634. Pai gow is played on a blackjack-style table with numbered seats. Before the deal, three dice are shaken to determine who will receive the first hand from the dealer. The dice are added together and the seats are counted out around the table until the number is reached and that player receives the first set of cards.

635. At each seat there is a square marked "high hand" and another marked "second high hand." The high hand is in the back, and the second high hand is in the front. It's easy to keep straight if you remember that two cards means "second high."

636. Each player is dealt seven cards, which he must arrange into a five-card hand and a two-card hand. The two-card hand goes face down in the front square (marked "second high") and the five-card hand goes face down in the back square (marked "high hand" on the table). The five-card hand (the high hand) must be a poker hand higher in ranking than the two-card hand.

637. After the players' hands are arranged, the dealer turns over his hand. The cards are then arranged into the two hands for the dealer. The casino has set rules about how the dealer's hand is to be arranged. This is called the "house way." After the dealers hand is set, the players' hands are turned over.

638. The player's front hand is matched against the dealer's front hand and the back hand is matched against the dealers back hand. In order to win, the player's two hands must beat the dealer's two hands. If one wins and one loses, it is a push.

PAI GOW STRATEGY

639. The skill in pai gow comes from setting the hands correctly. A good pai gow player can beat inexperienced players and this is why they prefer to act as the dealer when it is their turn to do so.

640. For all the strategy decisions listed on the following pages, the five-card hand will be called the back hand. The two card hand will be called the front hand. When a hand contains two or three sets of pairs, I refer to them as high pair, middle pair, or low pair according to their rank. This strategy is simplified, but will get you started if you want to give pai gow a try.

641. The setting of many hands will be determined by whether or not a player has an Ace or the joker in their hand. When the two-card hand contains an Ace (regardless of whether or not it is a pair), it has the potential of winning if the dealer does not have a pair in the front hand.

642. If you have no pair, you should put the highest card in the back. Put the second and third highest cards in the front hand. With a little luck, you may split by winning the front hand against the dealer's front hand.

643. If you have one pair, you should put the pair in the back hand and the two highest non-paired cards in the front hand.

644. If you have two pairs without an Ace, you should put the low pair in front and the high pair in back. If you have two pairs with an Ace, put the Ace in front with the highest no pair card and the two pairs in the back.

645. If you have three pairs, you should put the highest pair in the front and the middle and low pairs in the back. Your two pairs in back make a higher hand than your high pair in front. This gives you two powerful hands.

646. If you have three-of-a-kind, you will put the "trips" (the three-of-a-kind) in the back hand and your highest two cards in the front hand. The exception is if you have three Aces, then you would split them and put an Ace in front and the pair of Aces in the back.

647. If you have two sets of three-of-a-kind, place a pair from the higher three-of-a-kind in front. Place the lower three-of-a-kind in back. You want the higher pair in the front for strength.

648. If you have a straight, a flush, or a straight flush, keep the five cards together in your back hand unless you have a pair. If you can put the pair in front without breaking up the hand, then do so. If you can't, you should keep the five-card hand as-is in the back.

649. If you have a full house, you will break it up. Put the three-of-a-kind in the back hand. Put the pair in the front hand.

650. If you have four-of-a-kind without a single Ace in your seven cards, then break up the four into two pairs and put one pair in front and the other in the back hand. If you have a single Ace with the four-of-a-kind, keep the four together and put the Ace in front.

651. If you have five Aces (four Aces and the joker), place a pair of Aces in front and the remaining three Aces in the back. You won't see this hand too often, if ever.

ADVANTAGES OF PAI GOW

652. Pai gow is a slow game, so your money is not at risk much of the time. Since many hands end in a tie, it is even a better game to eat up the time while you collect your comps. For this reason you won't see many five-dollar tables, but it can actually be a better game to play than some of the other table games.

653. Be careful how you arrange the hands. If the front two-card hand is higher than the back five-card hand, the player automatically loses. If you are uncertain as to how to arrange the cards, you can have the dealer do it for you. Just turn you cards over and ask for the house way.

654. To act as the dealer, you must have a large enough bankroll to cover the other player's bets. Since you have a slight advantage as the dealer, you want to make sure to bring enough money to the table when you play to be able to bank the game.

Three-Card Poker

THE BASICS

655. Three-card poker was developed by Derek Webb of Great Britain. Shuffle Master, makers of the automated shuffling machine, owns the rights to the game outside of the British Isles. The game has become quite popular because it is easy to learn.

656. Three-card poker is a poker-derived game played with a fifty-two-card deck. Instead of receiving five or seven cards, the players are dealt only three. There are no additional cards drawn after the initial three cards are dealt.

657. Three-card poker is actually two games in one. The first game is the base game in which the player tries to beat the dealer with the better poker hand. This is the ante wager. With the ante wager, you are only betting that your hand will beat the dealer. You are not playing against the other players.

658. The second game is a wager made on whether you will be dealt a pair or better. This is called the pair plus game. The player can make separate wagers on either or both games. They can bet different amounts on either game.

659. In some casinos, you are required to make an ante bet in order to make the pair plus bet. Your pair plus bet cannot be higher than your ante wager. You should always check the rules before you sit down to play.

660. The game is played on a blackjack-sized table. There are three betting spots in front of each seat. The top betting spot is labeled "pair plus," where the player puts a wager on the pair plus game. Beneath that are two spots labeled "ante" and "play" for the base game.

THREE-CARD PLAY

661. Play begins with the player making a bet in the pair plus and/or ante spots. After all the players have made their bets, the dealer will give each player a three-card hand that is dealt by the Shuffle Master machine. Play begins with the first player to the dealer's left and continues clockwise around the table.

662. If the player has made a wager on the ante game, he must now make his decision to play or fold. If the player wants to continue with his hand, he must make a wager equal to his ante bet in the spot marked play. If the player does not want to continue, he folds his hand and forfeits the original ante bet.

663. After all the players have made their decisions, the dealer's hand is turned over. In order to play, the dealer's hand must qualify by having a Queen or better. If the dealer does not qualify, the player will be paid even money for their ante bet, but will not be paid for the play bet.

664. If the dealer does qualify, then the hands are compared to determine the winner. Because only three cards are used, the ranking of hands differs slightly from that of traditional poker hands. Following are the rankings for the three-card poker hands from highest to lowest.

665. **Straight Flush:** Three cards of the same suit in sequence. (Example: six, seven, and eight of spades.)
Three-of-a-Kind: Three cards of equal rank.
Straight: Three cards in sequence of mixed suits.
Flush: Three cards of the same suit
Pair: Two cards of equal rank.
High Card: The highest card in your hand.

666. Since you receive only three cards, there is no way you can make a full house, four-of-a-kind, or two pairs. A straight is higher than a flush because statistically you will be dealt three suited cards more frequently than three cards in sequence.

667. In the event of a tie, the player wins. This is rare because the third card can be used as a kicker to break the tie. For example, if both the player and dealer have a pair of Jacks, the one with the higher third card would win.

668. The strategy for the ante/play game is very simple. Fold unless you have Queen (Q), six, and four or better. This strategy results in a house edge of about 2 percent for the combined ante and play bets.

669. To determine if your hand is better than Queen, six, and four, start with your first highest card and compare it to the Queen. If it is higher, you play. You ignore the other two cards. If your first card is a Queen and your second card is higher than six, you would still play regardless of the ranking of your third card. If it is lower than six, you don't play.

670. Some published strategies tell you to mimic the dealer and play if you have a Queen or better without regards to the other two cards. Noted gaming mathematician Stanley Ko developed the more accurate strategy described here using the second and third cards.

671. Three-card poker offers an ante bonus that is paid based on your hand for the ante game. If you have a straight, three-of-a-kind, .or a straight flush, you will be paid a bonus regardless of whether the dealer qualifies.

672. The payout schedule for the ante bonus varies from casino to casino, but not by much. For a straight flush, you will be paid five to one or four to one. For three-of-a-kind, you will be paid four to one or three to one. For a straight, you receive one to one for your ante bet.

673. If the dealer does qualify and beats your hand, you are still entitled to the bonus payout. If you have three-of-a-kind and the dealer has a straight flush, you lose your ante and play bets, but still collect the ante bonus based on the payout schedule.

674. When you make a wager on the pair plus, you are betting that you will be dealt a pair or better. This bet is independent of the dealer's hand, even if you have a bet on the ante game and the dealer qualifies or beats you.

675. The pair plus bet is paid based on a set pay schedule. Like the pay table for the bonus payout, this pay schedule will vary from casino to casino. It is typical for the straight flush to pay forty to one and the pair to pay one to one. The variances come from the three-of-a-kind paying either thirty or twenty-five to one; the straight paying either six or five to one; and the flush paying either four or three to one.

676. You will be dealt a pair or better about 25 percent of the time, or once in every four hands. The house edge is affected by the pay schedule. With the best schedule, the house has about 2.3 percent edge over the player. Check the schedule before you sit down.

677. Three-card poker is one of the easiest games to play. It is a lot of fun to play and the pair plus bet is a lot better than the higher house edge you give up on the side bets for most other games.

THE BASICS

678. Four-card poker is another poker-based game that was developed by Roger Snow of Shuffle Master. It is played on the same type of table and utilizes the same Shuffle Master automatic shuffling machine that is used for three-card poker. There are some similarities and some distinct differences between the two games and their corresponding strategies.

679. Four-card poker is similar to three-card in that it is two games in one. The base game is the ante-play where you compete against the dealer. The second portion of the games is called "aces up" and is similar to the pair plus portion of three card.

680. The play begins with the player making independent wagers on either the aces up or ante portion of the game or both. The player can bet different amounts on each game if both games are played.

681. Although the game is called four-card poker, the player is dealt five cards face down and must make the best four-card hand. The dealer is dealt six cards, which are used to make the best four-card hand. One of the dealer's cards is dealt face up.

682. Four-card poker differs from three-card poker and Caribbean stud because the dealer does not have to qualify in order for the game to continue. After looking at your cards, you can fold and lose your ante bet or make an additional play bet to continue. You must at least match your ante bet, but you can elect to make a bet up to three times the amount of your original ante bet.

683. The ranking of hands for four-card poker also differs from the traditional five-card poker hands. The order is based on the mathematical frequency of hands and is made using just four of your five cards. Here are the rankings of hands:

Four-of-a-Kind
Straight Flush
Three-of-a-Kind
Flush
Straight
Two Pairs
Pair of Aces

684. If the player's hand beats the dealer's hand, the player wins the ante bet and the play bet. If the dealer wins the hand, the player loses both bets. In the event of a tie, the player will win. Ties are based on four cards only and the fifth card is never used to break a tie.

685. Four-card poker also offers an ante bonus. It is paid in addition to the ante and play bets, and is based on the player's hand for the ante game. If you have a three-of-a-kind, your are paid two to one. If you have a straight flush, you are paid twenty to one. If you have four-of-a-kind, you are paid twenty-five to one. You will be paid for the bonus regardless of whether the dealer beats your hand or not.

Four-Card Poker Strategy

686. If you decide to continue playing, you should bet either a single bet equal to your ante bet or three times your ante bet. Never bet two times your ante bet. You want to have as much money wagered when you have the advantage, which you will have when strategy dictates making the larger bet.

687. Shuffle Master has published a basic strategy that gives the players a 98.41 percent return on the game based for the combined ante/play and ante bonus.

- Bet three times your ante if you have a pair of tens or better.
- Bet the same amount as your ante if you have pairs of three through nine.
- Fold if you have less than a pair of threes.

688. Players will fold about 47 percent of the time. They will bet their ante 24 percent of the time. Players will bet three times their ante about 29 percent of the time. The player can expect to win about 70 percent of the time when they bet the maximum.

THE FOUR-CARD POKER ACES UP BET

689. The "aces up" bet is not affected by the dealer's hand. If the player has a pair of aces or better, they will be paid for the aces up bet based on the pay out schedule posted on the table. Even if you lose your ante bet, you can still collect for the aces up bet.

690. The pay table for the aces up bet varies from casino to casino. The most common payback has a house edge of 4.24 percent for this bet. It is as follows:

Four-of-a-kind	50 to 1
Straight flush	40 to 1
Three-of-a-kind	8 to 1
Flush	6 to 1
Straight	4 to 1
Two pairs	2 to 1
Aces	1 to 1

691. Four-card poker was designed to be a bit volatile. This means that you can experience some big swings in your bankroll. Most four-card poker players like the chance to win big and don't mind the added risks. If you stick to the ante/play portion of the game and play according to the basic strategy, it can be a good game.

Casino War

692. Casino war is the same game you probably played as a child before you were skilled enough to play more sophisticated games. The game is simple and fast, which makes it one of the easiest casino games to play.

693. The object of the game is to have a card that is higher than your opponent's is. In casino war, your opponent is the dealer. You are not playing against the other players at the table.

694. Casino war is played with six decks dealt out of a shoe. Cards are ranked as in poker, except Aces are always high. The suit does not matter.

695. The game starts with the player placing a wager in the betting circle. The player and dealer are each dealt one card face up. If the player's card is higher than the dealer's card, the player is paid even money for that bet. If the player's card is lower than the dealer's card, he loses.

696. The only decision the player has to make comes when there is a tie with the dealer's card. The player has two choices: to surrender and lose half his bet or to go to war with the dealer.

697. If you choose to go to war, you must put up an additional bet equal to your original bet. The dealer then burns (or discards) three cards and turns up one card for the player and one for the dealer. If your card is higher than the dealer's or ties the dealer's card for a second time, you win even money for your added bet and your original bet returned to you. If the dealer's card is higher, you lose both of your bets.

698. The rules of the game make it sound as if you will be winning two bets if you go to war and win, but this is not the case. When you go to war and win your original bet is returned to you (it is a push) and you are paid on the second bet that you put up to go to war. You really only win one bet when you beat the dealer but you lose two bets when he beats you.

699. The proper strategy is to always go to war in the event of a tie. The house edge when you go to war is 2.88 percent. When you surrender, the house has an edge of 3.70 percent. You are giving the house almost a full percent by not going to war.

700. There is one more bet that can be made in this game. Like baccarat, you can bet that there will be a tie. If you bet the tie and win it pays 10 to 1. This is a side bet that has a huge 18.65 percent house edge. It is a foolish bet and should be avoided.

Big Six Wheel

701. The big six wheel, which is also called the wheel of fortune or the money wheel, is easy to play and just as easy to lose. It is an old carnival game that is designed to separate the suckers from their money.

702. The standard big six wheel is about six feet across and is divided into nine sections with fifty-four individual stops. Fifty-two of the stops have dollar denominations and two of the stops have special symbols such as a joker and/or the casino logo.

703. The stops on the wheel are divided by pegs and are usually broken down as follows:
- Twenty-three one-dollar stops
- Fifteen two-dollar stops
- Eight five-dollar stops
- Four ten-dollar stops
- Two twenty-dollar stops
- Two logo or joker stops. The two logo spots pay forty or forty-five dollars, depending on the casino.

704. There is a glass-covered table in front of the wheel with corresponding symbols. You place your chip on top of the symbol you hope will win when the wheel is spun.

705. The wheel is spun by the dealer and a leather "flapper" mounted on top of the wheel clicks away hitting the stops. When it stops spinning, the flapper falls in between two pegs and indicates the winning number.

706. The house edge on every bet for this game is high. It runs between 11 percent on the one dollar spot to 24 percent on the logo or joker. This game should be avoided.

707. Many big six wheels are located at the exit or entrance to the casino. The casino hopes a player will drop down a dollar bet on the way in or out of the casino. Don't waste your money. Any game that originated at a carnival has "sucker" written all over it.

10.

Know When to Hold'em: Casino Poker

THE BASICS

708. Poker has recently become the most popular game in the casino. The card rooms are overflowing with players. It is a game of skill in which you are competing against the other players, not the house. If you want to be a winner, you must learn to play the game before you sit down at a table.

709. In poker, players compete against one another to win the money in the pot. (The pot is the money that is bet by the players during the hand.) A player can win in one of two ways. The first is to have the best five-card hand at the end of the game. The second way is to get your opponents to fold (give up their hands) with a series of bets or raises during the hand, making them think you have the best hand. This is known as bluffing.

710. Players of average intelligence can learn to be successful playing poker in the casinos if they take the time to educate themselves about the games. Poker tournaments on television make for great entertainment, but they are not the way to learn the game. If you are willing to spend the time and effort to learn and practice how to play correctly, you can play winning poker.

711. The three most popular poker games in the casino are Texas hold'em, 7-card stud, and Omaha. You can find all of these games played at various betting limits. There are low limit games for the novices and very high limit games for the professional players.

712. Regardless of which game you play, the biggest mistake a player can make is playing too many hands. The objective to poker is to win the most money. It is not to win the most pots. Players who win the most pots are playing too many hands and usually lose money in the end. A winning player is one who is very selective about the hands he or she plays. This takes patience and discipline, and it separates the winners from the losers.

713. The basic rules of any poker game are easy to learn, but to be a winning player you need more than just the basics. Poker is a game that combines math, psychology, and human emotions; an understanding of all three will help you win.

714. What makes poker a game of skill and separates it from most other casino games is that your decisions matter. In poker your decision to bet, call, raise, or fold will have an effect on the outcome. Although your objective is to make money, your main concern when you play poker is to always make the correct decisions.

Playing in a Casino Poker Room

715. Playing casino poker is quite different from playing in a home game. There are certain procedures and protocols you will need to understand before you sit down to play. Rules can vary from one card room to the next. If you are unsure of the rules, ask the dealer or floor person. Don't assume anything.

716. In a card room, you will find many players who are just out for a good time and don't play the game very well. Combined with what you know about poker strategy, their inexperience can be your gain.

717. You can't just take a seat at any poker table. You must first register at the card room's main desk when you enter. You will be notified when a seat is ready for you in the game you wish to play.

718. The casinos make their money by taking a small amount out of each pot. This is called the rake. The amount of the rake can vary with the limits of the game you are playing and can change from one poker room to the next. Look for the casino taking the smallest rake.

719. In a poker room, the dealer only deals the cards and does not play in the game. A small white disk with the word "dealer" printed on it will rotate around the table clockwise to denote who will act last. This disk is called the button.

720. Don't throw your chips into the pot; always place your bet in front of you. This way the dealer sees that your bet is correct. Once, he or she has checked it, they will add it to the pot.

721. If you are going to raise, you should announce "raise" when it is your turn. If you don't announce a raise, you must put in the bet and the raise in at the same time. If you put in the bet first and then go back to your stack for the raise, you will be called for a "string bet," which is not allowed, and your raise will not be honored.

722. It is up to each player to protect his cards at all times. Place your hands or a chip on top of your cards. If other players' cards mix with yours when they throw in their cards, your hand will be declared dead.

723. If you expose your cards during a hand either intentionally or by mistake, it is considered a dead hand. Make sure all betting is complete before you turn your cards over. There is nothing worse than forfeiting the winning hand because of not paying attention to the action at the table.

724. You must pay attention to the amount of the bet made by the first active player. You have to know what the bet is when it is your turn. You must also be aware if someone has raised the bet.

725. Don't fold your hand if you can check. If everyone else checks, you get to see the next card for free. It might be the card that can turn your hand into a winner.

726. The cards speak for themselves. Don't immediately throw in your cards if someone calls out a better hand. The dealer will declare the winner of the hand.

727. It is against the rules to act out of turn. Doing so can give the other players an unfair advantage. Make sure to wait until it is your turn to act. Even if you plan to fold, you have to wait.

728. When it is your turn to act, do so as quickly as possible. This will keep the game moving. If you are unsure or need an extra minute to decide, you can say "time please" and you will be given time to make your decision.

729. In casino poker, you play for table stakes. This means that you play with the chips that you have on the table. You're not allowed to go into your pocket for more money in the middle of a hand.

730. If you run out of chips, you announce that you are "all in" and you will only be eligible for the money in the pot up to that point. Any additional bets made by others will be put in a side pot. You will not be eligible for this pot even if you have the best hand. Instead, the side pot goes to the player with the highest hand amongst the players who put money in the side pot.

731. You can get up and leave the table to go to the bathroom, stretch your legs, or take a break for any other reason. What you can't do is take your chips with you if you plan to return to the game. Leave your chips on the table when you take a break.

732. When you are first seated at a table, you may not have a choice of seats unless it is a new game. This does not mean you can't change your seat once you are in the game. If a player is leaving the table, you can request his seat by telling the dealer as soon as you see him get ready to go.

733. "Check raising" is when you check your hand and then raise after another player bets after you. In home games, the idea of check raising is considered sandbagging and is frowned upon or even not allowed. It is allowed in most casino poker rooms and is a powerful tool to help you extract more money from your fellow players.

734. The most important decision you will make is made before you even leave your house. That decision is whether or not to play poker. If you are not prepared to play your best game and devote your full attention to your play, then you should stay away from the poker table. Your attitude and frame of mind can and will affect your decisions at the table.

735. Make it a habit to look at your hole cards (your face down cards) once and memorize them. This will allow you to act quickly when it is your turn and keep the game going. It will also prevent you from giving away any tells (hints about the cards you are holding) that may occur by looking at your cards.

736. You should have a game plan before you sit down at the table. Mental preparation can be just as critical as knowing the selection of hands you will play. Get enough rest and eat properly before playing. This will help you stay alert during the game.

737. Game selection is very important. You don't have to be the best player in the world. You only have to be better than the others at the table. If your opponents are too tough, then you should find an easier game.

738. Study the other players to determine what type of players they are. After some time at the table, you should be able to determine whether a player is loose or tight. You should also have an idea of the types of hands they play.

739. Review and analyze your own play after each session. No matter how good you think you are, there is always room to improve your game. You can only do this through honest assessment of your play.

740. Bad players are profitable and you want them in the game. Never berate or try to educate another player at the table. If you suffer a bad beat, just say "nice hand" and move on. If you berate a bad player, you may drive them out of the game. If you educate them, they may play better next time.

741. Make sure that you bring to the table at least twenty times the amount of the table's maximum bet to gamble with. Playing when you are under capitalized is not the way to play winning poker. You want to make sure you have enough to handle the loss of a hand without having to buy more chips.

742. Never try to bluff more than two players at once. There will usually be someone who wants to "keep you honest." In low limit games if there is even one calling station at your table, you should not bluff. (A calling station is a player who will not fold his hand and will stay in the hand to the end.)

743. If the pot is raised before it is your turn to act, you will have to call the original bet and the raise. This is known as cold calling. Unless you have a very powerful hand, you should fold. You need a stronger hand to call a raise than you do to initiate one.

744. Keep your emotions in check. The table is not the place for foul language or temper tantrums. It will not be tolerated, and it makes you look foolish.

745. If you start to get tired, leave the game. Playing winning poker takes concentration. If you play too long, you may get tired or even bored. This can cause you to make mistakes or play marginal hands.

Tells

746. The term "tell" is short for a telltale sign. It can be a voluntary movement that a player makes to try to deceive you or it can be an involuntary reaction to the cards. If you can learn to spot tells, you will be able to win some hands just by reading another player.

747. Most players will act strong when they are weak and act weak when they are strong. A player who looks sad or shrugs when placing chips into the pot usually has a very strong hand.

748. A player staring right at you is trying to intimidate you and is daring you to call their bet. They usually have a weak hand or are bluffing. A player looking away from you, trying to seem uninterested usually has a strong hand. That player wants you to call.

749. If a player's hands are shaking when they make their bet, you can be sure that they have a very strong hand. This is an involuntary tell that is usually not an act.

750. If a player looks at their chips after seeing the dealer turn over the community cards in hold'em or the next card dealt to them in 7-card stud, it usually means they are going to bet. For most players, this involuntary action signifies they like what they see.

751. In Texas hold'em, if a player looks at his pocket cards when three cards of the same suit flop (first three community cards), they usually don't have a flush. Chances are they have one card of that suit and they want to see the value of the suited card.

752. After the flop in Texas hold'em, a player staring at the flop usually was not helped by it. A player who sees the flop and immediately looks away or glances down at their chips has made a hand.

753. When you first sit down at a table, study the way the players stack their chips. Although it is a generalization, loose aggressive players typically maintain unorganized/sloppy stacks, while tight conservative players keep well organized/neat stacks.

754. A player who is very attentive and sitting in an erect position usually has a strong hand. A player who bluffs a lot leans forward in a confrontational way. Remember, strong is weak!

755. Watch how the players make their bets. A player forcibly throwing chips into the pot usually does not have a strong hand. Players try to act strong when they are weak and throwing chips is usually a sign of this.

11.

Know When to Fold'em: Texas Hold'em

THE BASICS

756. Texas hold'em is the most popular poker game in the world. It is fast paced, and easy to learn. The game can be played with more players than can 7-card stud, which means bigger pots, making it very exciting and quite profitable for those players who make the effort to learn to play correctly.

757. Each player is dealt two personal cards face down ("hole" cards), and five community cards are dealt face up in the middle of the table. The players will use any combination of their two hole cards and the five community cards to form the best five-card poker hand. Since there are five community cards, you do not have to keep track of all the dead cards that were folded by your opponents as you do in 7-card stud.

758. Texas hold'em is a faster paced game than 7-card stud. You can play a hand in about two minutes. This means you will see more hands during your playing session. This allows you to be more selective, which should lead to profitability if you capitalize on the poor playing of your opponents.

759. The Texas hold'em tournaments you see on television are no-limit Texas hold'em games. That means that at any time a player can bet all of his chips. This is a great format for tournaments, but as a beginning player, you should first learn to play limit Texas hold'em.

760. Limit hold'em games have structured betting rounds that limit the amount of money you can bet during each round. You will want to play low-limit Texas hold'em as you learn the game. Some of the low limit games you will find in the card room have a betting structure of $2-$4, $3-$6, $4-$8.

761. After you gain experience, you can move up to higher limits or no limit if you desire. You need to learn how to beat the lower limit games before you move up. You will usually find more skilled players in the higher limit games.

762. In Texas hold'em, there are four betting rounds. In a $2-$4 limit game, for example, the minimum bet during the first two betting rounds is two dollars. If you want to raise, you must raise in increments of two dollars. The last two betting rounds have a minimum bet of four dollars, and any raises are made in this increment as well.

763. To start a new hand, two blind bets are put up or "posted." The player immediately to the left of the dealer posts the small blind, which is half the minimum bet for the first betting round. The player to the left of the small blind posts the big blind, which is equal to the minimum bet. In a $2-$4 game, the small blind would be one dollar, and the big blind would be two dollars.

764. In many casinos a new player sitting down at the Texas hold'em table has to post a bet equal to the big blind if he wishes to be dealt into the next hand. This is not mandatory and you may elect to wait until it is your turn to be the big blind before you enter the game.

765. Each player is dealt two cards face down with the player on the small blind receiving the first card and the player with the dealer button getting the last card. The first betting round is known as the pre-flop and begins with the player to the left of the big blind either putting in two dollars (in a $2-$4 game) to call the blind bet, putting in four dollars to raise the big blind, or folding his hand.

766. The betting moves around the table in order until it reaches the player who posted the small blind. Unless there has been a raise that player can call (or match) the bet by putting in one dollar, since a dollar blind was already posted or fold. The last person to act is the big blind. If no one has raised the pot, the dealer will ask if he or she would like the option. This means the big blind has the option to raise the bet by adding more chips or just check.

767. By checking, the big blind does not put in any more money. Because the big blind is actually the first bet of the new hand, the player with the big blind has already made his bet. Some new players make the mistake of throwing their cards if they don't like their hand. This common mistake should be avoided.

768. The pile of discarded hands is called the muck. Players refer to folding their hands as mucking their cards. Don't throw your cards into the pile. Push them forward on the table and the dealer will move them into the muck pile. Never show your cards to another player before folding your hand.

769. If you are not one of the players posting (putting up money for) the blinds, it will not cost you any money to see your two starting cards. You can afford to be selective and wait for good starting hands. Playing inferior starting cards is the biggest and most common mistake made by losing players.

THE FLOP

770. After the first betting round is completed, three community cards are dealt and turned face up in the middle of the table. This is known as the flop. Another betting round begins with the first active player to the left of the dealer button. The minimum bet for this round is again two dollars in a $2-$4 game.

771. The flop defines your hand because after the flop you will have seen five cards or 5/7 of the final hand, which is equal to 71 percent. At this point, you need to assess your hand and decide whether or not to continue.

772. There are 19,600 three-card combinations that can be made with the three flop cards. When you add in your two personal cards, 2,598,960 five-card combinations can be made. If the flop did not improve your hand, then chances are it improved the hand of one of your opponents.

THE TURN

773. When the betting round after the flop is completed, the dealer turns a fourth card face up in the middle of the table. This is referred to as the turn or fourth street. The minimum bet after the turn is now double the limit of the first two betting rounds (four dollars in a $2-$4 game). The play begins again with the first active player to the left of the dealer.

THE RIVER

774. Following the betting round for the turn, the dealer will turn over a fifth and final card (called the river), and the final betting round begins. When the betting is finished, the players turn over their two hole cards to determine the winner.

775. To determine the winner, the players may use any combination of their two hole cards and the five cards on the board (table) to form the highest five-card hand. In some rare cases, the best hand will be the five cards on board.

PRE-FLOP

776. Position is probably the most overlooked concept involved in playing winning Texas hold'em. Your position is determined by where you are sitting in relationship to the dealer's button. Unlike 7-card stud, where the betting order changes with each betting round, the order is fixed in Texas hold'em.

777. Before the flop, the person to the left of the big blind bets first. After the flop, the first active player to the left of the dealer button acts first. If you are in early position, you will remain there for all betting rounds. (Even though the blinds make their decision last before the flop, the have actually acted first by posting the blind bets.)

778. There are seven positions in a ten-handed hold'em game (that is, a game with ten players).

Small Blind: Player posting small blind

Big Blind: Player posting big blind

Under the Gun (UTG): Player who acts first after the big blind

Early: The two players after UTG

Middle: The two players after Early

Late: The two players after Middle

Button: The player with the dealer button

779. You need a stronger hand to play from early position because you have more players acting after you who may raise or re-raise the pot. It is important that you are patient and wait for the right starting hands to play from the correct position.

780. You can be dealt 169 two-card combinations before the flop. Hands of equal rank but different suits are counted as one because they have the same value before the flop. Of these 169 hands, only about seventy-five are playable, and not all of them can be played from every position.

781. There is no set mathematical strategy for stating hands as there is in blackjack. Each game is different based on the players and type of game. You can follow some general guidelines for determining which hands you should play based on your position.

782. In Early position: Raise with A-A, K-K, and A-Ks (s denotes suited cards). Call with A-K, A-Qs, K-Qs, Q-Q, J-J, and T-T. Fold everything else.

783. In Middle position, add the following hands: call with 9-9, 8-8, A-Js, A-Ts, Q-Js, A-Q, and K-Q. Fold everything else or if there is a raise.

784. In Late position, add the following hands: call with A-Xs, K-Ts, Q-Ts, J-Ts, A-J, A-T, and small pairs. Fold everything else or if there is a raise. (X denotes any card.)

785. It takes a stronger hand to call a raise than it does to initiate one. If there is a raise before it is your turn to act, you should fold your weaker hands. Why put in two bets with a marginal hand?

786. Many players will play any two suited cards from any position and play an Ace with any small kicker (an unpaired card used to break a tie). These hands are losers in the long run and you should avoid getting into the habit of playing them. They are traps that will cost you money.

FLOP STRATEGY

787. You can tell the best possible hand by looking at the community cards. Although it is not certain that one of your opponents will actually have the best hand, you can assess the strength of your hand in relation to the best theoretical hand and determine if you have a chance of winning the pot. This is known as reading the board.

788. In poker, your outs are the unseen cards that will complete or improve your hand to make it the winning hand. Each additional card or "out" will improve your percentage of making the winning hand.

789. Your skills at reading your opponents and reading the board are important when figuring your outs. You need to assess your opponents' hands and try to determine what they may have. Your perception of their hands will form the basis for deciding what you need to beat them.

790. The rule of four-two is an easy way to get a quick, ballpark figure of the percentage for making a hand. With two cards to come after the flop, you multiply your number of outs by four. With one card to come after the turn, you multiply your number of outs by two.

791. Many players use the fit or fold criteria for deciding to play after the flop. If the flop does not fit your hand, you should fold if there is a bet in front of you. A flop fits your hand by improving it or by giving you a good draw to improve your hand, or simply if your hand beats the cards on the board as it is.

792. If you saw the flop with a small pair and did not improve by making a set (three-of-a-kind), you should fold if there are higher cards on the flop and there has been a bet and/or a raise in front of you. There are only two cards that will improve your hand and the odds are eleven to one against you on the turn and twenty-two to one against you on the river.

793. If the pot is small, you should fold marginal hands. You are not getting correct odds to attempt a draw to an inside straight. If there are only one or two players and the pot is raised, playing this hand is unprofitable.

794. Any time you have top pair (one of your hole cards matches the highest card on the board) and a four-card flush, draw after seeing the flop; you have a very strong hand. Be aggressive when you play this hand. You want to increase the size of the pot. If you don't make your flush, there is a chance your pair will win.

795. Semi-bluffing is done when your hand is not strong enough to win the pot at the time, but has the chance of improving to the best hand. If you bet or raise, you are hoping that the other players will fold and you will win the pot without going any further. If you are called, then you still have a chance that your hand will improve to be the best hand. Raising with four cards to a flush after the flop is a good example of when to semi-bluff.

796. Slow playing is a term used to describe when you play a strong hand weakly. This is done to build the pot when a bet or a raise may cause other players to fold. For example, if you have a full house after the flop, you want to get the other players to stay in. You would only call the bets rather than raise. If you are first to act, you would check so another player might think you have a weak hand.

Turn Strategy

797. When a player raises the flop, but then checks after the turn card, it usually means they have a drawing hand (one that needs additional cards to make it the winner). The raise on the flop was most likely an attempt to get the other players to check to the raiser. When this happens the raiser can also check and get to see the next card for free without having to bet. Read the board carefully to look for flush or straight possibilities.

798. If you think you have the best hand after seeing the turn card and are first to act, then go ahead and bet. Many players will try to get fancy and attempt to check raise in this position. If the other players also check, you have lost a bet or two.

799. If you get to the turn and you hold only two unsuited over cards (two cards higher than any cards on the board) with no flush or straight draw, then you should fold if there is a bet in front of you. Too much money is lost by players who hope to catch a miracle card on the river. The best hand you can make with two unsuited over cards is a pair, which will probably lose anyway.

River Strategy

800. Do not fold in large pots on the river for one bet. Bad players often like to bluff with hopeless hands on the river. If you call and lose, it will cost you one bet. If you fold a winner, you have lost many bets.

801. Many players will bluff on the river if they did not make their draw. Read the board carefully. If there are not three suited cards on the board, no one can make a flush. If there is not a pair on the board, no one can have four-of-a-kind or a full house.

802. If you have been playing properly, you will not see the river card unless you have a strong hand that is a favorite to win or you have a draw to a winning hand. Once the river card is turned over, you know exactly what you have. If you were drawing to a hand, you know whether you were successful or not. Of course, if you do not make your hand, you will fold.

803. Never show your hand if you don't have to. If everyone folds and you win the pot, don't show your hand. When you show your hand, you are giving away valuable information.

TYPES OF PLAYERS

804. You will encounter all types of players in the poker room. You will find that most players will fall into a few common categories based on what hands they play and how they play their hands at the table. Players can be loose or tight and passive or aggressive.

805. Loose players believe that any two cards can win. They have no set standard as to which hands they play and will try to play as many hands as possible. They want to be involved and once they are in the hand, they are reluctant to fold.

806. Tight players are just the opposite of loose players. They are very selective about the hands they play. They will only play premium hands that will have the best chance of winning. They prefer to play starting hands with large cards and pocket pairs.

807. Passive players like to check and call. They don't like to raise and they will play their hands without much conviction. They won't push their hands by raising, preferring to let other players dictate the action.

808. Aggressive players will play their hands strongly. They will raise when the opportunity presents itself. They like to control the action, preferring to bet or raise rather than check or call. They are not afraid to check raise or cap the betting to eliminate other players.

809. A loose passive player is known as a calling station. They will play many hands, but will not play them strongly. A calling station will cold call two raises before the flop and stay until the river, looking for that miracle draw. Even if it is clear that they are beaten, they will sometimes call just to keep you honest or to see what you had.

810. A loose aggressive player is referred to as the maniac. The maniac never saw a hand they couldn't raise with. The maniac craves action and wants as much of it as possible; they will play many hands and will bet and raise at every opportunity.

811. The maniac is the player you want to have sitting on your right so you can fold your weaker hands when they go into action. When the maniac is sitting on your left, you never know if they are going to raise you as soon as you bet. You will have to play tighter when the maniac is to your left.

812. You should strive to become a tight aggressive player. This player is very selective about the hands he or she plays, but will not hesitate to raise and control the action when they do play a hand.

813. Many players will sit in a game for hours, but be unable to give you any specifics about their opponents. The only way you will be able to determine the type of player you are up against is by studying them during the game. You should spend your time observing the other players when you are not involved in the hand.

814. A winning player is one who initiates the action. If you are first to act, rather than checking, you should bet. If there is a bet before you, consider raising rather than calling. You should be well aware of the complete arsenal at your disposal including check raising, slow playing, semi-bluffing, and how to gain a free card if necessary.

815. You should always be aware of the number of players involved in the hand. Was there a raise before the flop? If so, who raised and what type of hands has that person been playing? You should also be aware of the pot odds and ask yourself if the odds justify calling a bet or raise.

12.

Follow the
Bouncing Ball:
Live and Video Keno

THE BASICS

816. Keno is a game similar to the lottery in which players choose numbers that are then compared to a set of numbers drawn at random. The more numbers the players match, the more money they win.

817. Although there is no written history of origin of the game of keno, it is generally agreed that the game was introduced by Chéung Léung of the Han Dynasty as a way of supporting the army when provisions were failing. The game became known as "White Dove" because they used doves to carry the results across the county.

818. Chinese immigrants (who came to work on the railroads or in the gold and silver mines) brought keno to the United States in the mid- to late-1800s. The game was referred to as the Chinese lottery.

819. During the Depression, a game similar to the Chinese lottery was started in Montana. The game was called the lottery and appealed to people looking for a big return on a small investment. Since gambling was illegal in Montana, the game found its way to Nevada, where gambling was legal.

820. Lotteries were illegal in Nevada as well, but keno, which was then the name for the game we now call bingo, was legal. The lottery game was adapted and called race horse keno. The names of race horses were printed next to the numbers on the tickets and each drawing was called a race.

821. Around 1951, Nevada passed a law taxing off-track betting operations. The names of the race horses were taken off the tickets to avoid the tax. To this day, keno games are still referred to as races.

822. Numbers on the keno ticket were picked by brushing ink onto the ticket to make a spot over the numbers. The marking was called a spot and this term is used today to refer to a number picked on the keno ticket.

823. Catching a number or catching a spot is the term used for matching one of your numbers to that of a winning number drawn. You will usually hear the term "catch" used throughout the lounge and even in promotions such as a catch-six promotion where you receive a bonus for a winning six for six ticket.

824. Keno is a game that is based purely on luck. There is no skill required and nothing you can do to change the house edge. It is the equivalent to playing the lottery.

825. It is easier to win if you select fewer numbers. You get the best odds you can get in a keno game by picking a single number. Avoid picking more than nine numbers on a straight-up ticket. The more numbers you pick, the higher the odds become.

826. Live keno has the highest house edge of any game offered by the casino. It can be 25 percent or higher, depending on the payouts offered. Compare payouts from different casinos and play at the one offering the best payouts.

How to Play

827. Keno is played with eighty numbered balls. In each game, twenty out of the eighty will be drawn. The numbers are matched to the spots on the player's ticket. The winners are paid based on the pay table for the number of winning spots that are drawn for that game.

828. There are eighty numbers printed on each keno slip, arranged in eight rows of ten. These numbers correspond to the eighty numbered casino balls that are used in the drawing. The player marks the numbers that they think will be drawn during the game. The player takes this to the casino writer who issues a computer-generated ticket for the next game.

829. Check your printed ticket carefully to make sure it matches the numbers you chose on your keno slip. If a mistake is made and not corrected by the time the game starts, it can't be changed. If the number you chose wins but your ticket is incorrect, you lose.

830. The numbered keno balls are drawn out of a large, clear bowl device called a gooseneck or goose. One keno writer will call out the number printed on the ball and another will post that number on the large electronic display. There are numerous display boards situated around the casino and other areas such as restaurants and lounges.

831. Live keno is a very slow game. It takes about thirty seconds to draw the numbers, and about two minutes passes between races. This means you will only see about twelve contests per hour.

832. On a straight ticket, the player picks between one and fifteen spots. They are paid for each winning number drawn that corresponds to the spots on their ticket. Depending on the number of spots picked, you may be paid if only some of your numbers are picked.

833. All keno lounges have printed brochures that will show you how to fill out a ticket. The brochure will list all the pay-offs for a straight ticket and show you payouts for any specialty games that are offered.

834. Many casinos still have keno lounges where a player can go to make their bets and watch the winning numbers drawn. Most casinos have keno stations scattered around the casino where you can make your bet. You can bet single games or make advance wagers on multiple drawings from any keno station.

835. You must redeem winning single game tickets before the next game begins. You must redeem winning multi-game tickets written for twenty games or less at the end of the last game, but before the next game begins. Winning multi-game tickets for more than twenty games can be redeemed up to a year after the last game is called.

836. Way tickets have groups of two or more numbers that are bet on the same ticket. The groups are circled or separated with lines to provide two or more wagers on the same ticket. The groups can be combined or bet separately. A group of two and a group of three on the same ticket can be bet as one two-number bet, one three-number bet, or combined to form a five-number bet.

837. One number grouped by itself on a way ticket is called a king. The single number can be combined with the other groups on the ticket. You may have more than one king on a ticket.

838. Some casinos offer keno games with a progressive jackpot. These games require the player to pick twenty numbers. The progressive jackpot is usually paid to players hitting fourteen numbers or more. Rules may vary and you should check them before playing.

839. A player can bet any amount on a ticket as long as they meet the minimum bet, which is a dollar in most casinos. The minimum amount on a way ticket is less because the number of bets on the ticket is divided by the money bet and it works out to less than a dollar a bet.

840. There is no change in the house edge if you bet a way ticket. Your odds of catching your numbers are the same. You could just as easily bet them as individual tickets. Some players prefer to have all the bets on one ticket, in which case the way ticket is best.

841. A keno runner is an employee of the casino who will take your marked keno ticket and place your bet for you. They also can collect the winnings and bring them back to the players. In Las Vegas, there are keno runners in the restaurants and other areas to take your bets for you.

842. Many players will replay the same number over and over. If you want to do this, you can retain your original keno slip and hand it to the writer or runner. They will issue you a new ticket for the next game.

843. Avoid playing a lot of "Birthday numbers." Keno uses eighty numbers, which means if you use numbers associated with special dates you are limiting yourself to a small fraction of the available numbers. Try some different number that will include the ones in the higher range.

844. If you are not sure which numbers to bet, you can ask for a quick pick. The computer will generate the numbers for you.

845. The more numbers you pick, the higher the odds become. Avoid picking more than nine numbers for straight bet. The odds of hitting nine for nine is 1,380,358 to 1.

Video Keno

846. Video keno offers the player better odds than live keno. Because it is considered a slot machine, it must pay back at least the minimum of the other slot machines as determined by the local laws. Because the odds of hitting any number of spots don't change in live or video keno, the paybacks for the games are altered by changing the pay schedule.

847. The minimum bet for video keno is less than live keno. Instead of betting a dollar per game, you can bet a quarter. Some casinos even offer video keno for a nickel a play.

848. Video keno is much faster than live keno, and it only takes a few seconds to play a game. Because you can play more games per hour, it increases your chance of winning. It also increases your chance of losing, but at a quarter a game, the small wins can keep you going.

849. A keno machine played at the maximum of eight games a minute for one quarter bet will cycle through $120 per hour. With a house edge of 7.5 percent, the theoretical loss for the player is nine dollars per hour, betting a quarter a game.

850. Video keno is easy to play. Deposit one to four coins or put your money in the bill receptor. Press the clear button to clear off the screen and you are ready to go. Make your picks then hit the start button.

851. Video keno is usually limited to picking a maximum of ten spots. Once you've made your selection, the machine will light up twenty random numbers, one at a time. There is a help screen that will show you the pay table for the number of spots that you picked.

852. Many players will replay the same numbers until they win. If you want to replay them, just hit the start button. If you want new numbers, you will have to hit the clear button before picking your new numbers.

853. Limit the number of spots you pick to increase your chances of winning. Your best bet is to choose between three and eight spots per game. The odds of hitting eight for eight is 230,000 to 1, but you don't have to hit all eight to win.

854. Like video poker, the pay tables for video keno can vary from casino to casino. The number of winning spots needed to collect payment may change as well. For example, if you pick eight spots, you may get paid something if you hit five, six, seven, or eight spots on one machine, but only get paid if you hit six, seven, or eight on a machine with a different pay schedule.

855. Read the pay table on the machine before making your bet. Remember the payouts and try to keep your winnings below what you have to pay taxes on. Keep your bets to a maximum payout of $1,175. Then you can take your money home and you don't have to worry about old Uncle Sam.

856. Don't play a single spot. Whether you play live or video keno, you should avoid playing a singe spot. The percentages of hitting that one spot are too much against you for the small potential win you will collect.

857. The probability of hitting a royal flush in video poker is about forty thousand to one. You will be paid four thousand coins when you bet five. The odds of hitting seven out of seven spots on video keno machine are about forty-one thousand to one. You will get paid seven thousand coins for a one-coin bet. This may vary with the pay schedule, but keno payout can be greater than the video poker payout.

858. Unless you are playing a progressive machine, you should stick to one coin. If you want to bet more than a quarter, play a single coin on the dollar machine. You want to stretch your playing bankroll and you are not penalized for playing single coins as you are with regular slots that have a bonus for maximum coin play.

859. Video keno payouts are usually listed as a dollar value and not as machine credits. This can help you manage your money because you can see a real dollar amount attached to your credits. If you hit a big jackpot, make sure to lock up a win by setting a stop loss or, better yet, cash out your winnings and start over, putting less money in the machine.

860. Some players see patterns formed from the winning numbers. They think that they can predict a winner from these patterns. Since the numbers are generated at random, there is no way to determine a winner from the past games.

13.

Be a Sport: Sports Betting

THE BASICS

861. In the United States, sports betting is only legal in the state of Nevada, but more wagering is done on sporting events than any other form of gambling. Offshore sports sites, illegal bookmaking operations, office pools, and bets amongst friends and sports fans make it the number one gambling activity.

862. Individuals who wager on sports are sometimes called players. This term becomes confusing because the ones actually participating in the sport are also called the players. The word "punter" is used to describe a sports bettor in most other parts of the world.

863. The term wiseguy refers to large bettors or betting syndicates who are very knowledgeable. Money bet by the wiseguys is called smart money and the bets are often big enough to change the odds on the sporting event.

864. The casinos make their money on sports bets by collecting a commission on every losing bet made. This is called the vigorish, or vig for short. Ideally they would like to have the same amount wagered on both teams so that the losing bets cover the winning bets and the casino's money is untouched. To accomplish this they assign a handicap to the favorite team in the form of a point spread or money odds to make the event equally attractive for each side. This handicap is called the line.

865. The point spread is not the odds maker's predicted margin-of-victory. It is his prediction of what odds will be required to split the wagering evenly on both teams. For this reason, the line may change from the opening line to the line at game time.

866. There are two types of betting lines used in sports betting. The money line and the point spread. The point spread is commonly used in football, basketball, and hockey. The money line can also be bet in football, but is more common to baseball and boxing.

867. The area in the casino where you wager on sporting events is called the sports book. In the sports book you will find the display with all the events on which you can wager. This is called the board and in most of the bigger casinos, it is an electronic display; however, it might be handwritten in the smaller casinos.

868. The board is divided into sections that are organized by the sports being played at that time of the year. All the teams are listed on the board with a game reference number preceding the team name. When you place a bet, you have to use this number and not the team name.

869. Most sports books also have sheets of paper listing the games, the odds, and point spreads. Since the sheets are printed in advance, the odds listed on the sheet may change. The game numbers will be accurate, but you should update the lines from the board.

870. For the team sports such as football, baseball, basketball, and hockey, the teams are listed on the board in pairs for each game that is being played. The home team is listed on the bottom and the visiting team is on the top. If the game is being played at a neutral site, it may be noted with an asterisk.

871. For football and baseball, one of the teams will have a small number after it, denoting the point spread. The other team will have a larger number next to it, which is the total score of the game. The favored team has the smaller number next to it and this is always a negative number, although they do not put the minus sign before it.

872. When you bet on a game with the point spread, your team does not necessarily have to win. You just need to "cover the spread." If you bet Miami, who is favored to win by seven, and they only win by four, you lose; if Miami wins by seven or more, you win. If you bet Chicago, who is a ten-point underdog, and they only lose by three points, then you win; if they lose by ten points or more, you lose.

873. When you make a money line bet, you are wagering a larger bet on the favorite to win less money or a smaller bet on the underdog to win more money. The odds are given in relationship to one hundred dollars. If the line is +150/-140, you would have to bet 140 on the favorite to win 100 or 100 on the underdog to win 150.

874. For baseball, a money line is used and sometimes a run line is used as well. The line in baseball is determined by the starting pitchers for the game. The pitchers will be listed next to each team. If a non-listed pitcher starts for either team, the bets are cancelled.

875. The run line is used in baseball when one team is a big favorite. A number of runs, such as one and a half or two, are subtracted from the score of the favorite team. This is similar to the point spread in football.

876. Hockey games are usually bet using the money line as well. They will be listed on the board in a similar fashion as baseball games. If one team is a big favorite, there may be a puck line listed. This is like the run line in baseball and a goal or two would be subtracted from the favorite or added to the underdog.

877. When you make a point spread bet you are betting eleven to win ten. This is known as laying or giving the odds. When you make a point spread bet, you will be paid ten when you win, but it will cost you eleven if you lose. The dollar is the vig that the casino collects.

878. A straight bet is a bet made on a single game or outcome. You can choose to bet the favorite or the underdog. Depending on the sport, it will be either a spread bet or a money line bet.

879. In a straight bet, you can also choose the over or the under for the game total. Betting the over or the under is a bet on the total score at the end of the game. You add the scores of both teams to get the final number. When you bet the under, you are betting that the score will be under the total. When you bet the over, you are betting the score will be higher than the total.

880. A parlay bet is a single bet that links together the outcome of two different events. The parlay can be comprised of a series of bets on a team, over/under bets, or any mixture of the two. For the parlay to be a winning wager, every one of its individual plays must win. If any of the individual plays is not a winner, then the entire parlay wager loses.

881. Parlay bets are attractive because the bet is low and the payoff is high; however, you have to pick multiple winners to be successful. It might be to your advantage to pick several games straight up instead of linking them together.

882. Parlay cards are very popular with the recreational players because they have a minimum bet of one or two dollars. The cards have twenty or more games listed and you pick three or more games to win. You usually have to pick a minimum of three games.

883. The payoffs for parlay cards are listed on the back. Make sure you read the card carefully. On some parlay cards, you lose if one or more of your teams tie. These cards should be avoided.

884. A teaser can only be played in football and basketball. The teaser is one wager consisting of two or more propositions in which you are allowed to adjust the point spread in your favor. You do this by subtracting points from the point spread if you bet the favorite or adding points to the spread if you are betting on the underdog. For example, in a two-team football teaser you can add or subtract six and a half points to the point spread of each team. Most teasers are even money bets.

885. A futures bet is made on an event or outcome that is far off in the distance, such as a football team winning the Super Bowl or a baseball team winning the World Series. Because so much can change from the time of the bet to the actual time of the event, making a winning futures bet is very difficult.

886. A proposition bet is a very specific bet offered by the house. The individual bets have titles that explain what event, action, or player the wager is being placed on. Proposition bets are always money line bets. An example of a proposition bet is which team will score first during the Super Bowl.

Tips

887. Always make sure to double check your betting slips before leaving the window. If a mistake was made, it cannot be corrected once you walk away. You must alert the cashier immediately, and he or she will issue you a new ticket.

888. Sometimes betting lines may vary from casino to casino. Shop around to find the best number for the game you want to bet. Lines at different sports books can vary by as much as a point or more. The lines you see listed in the paper may not be the same lines as the sports book, but they are good to use for comparison.

889. The Federal Wire Act made it illegal to transmit gaming information by phone. Because of this, you are not allowed to use a cell phone in the sports book area of the casino. If you are seen making a call, you will be asked to hang up or leave the area.

890. Many factors determine the point spread—past performance, injuries, weather, where the game is being played, whether a team has been hot recently, etc. Always check the weather and injuries on game day before placing your bets. You can find all of this information on the Internet, in your local newspaper, or on any of the televised pre-game shows.

891. The odds maker sets the lines on how they believe the public will bet. They are not set on which team should win. This is a very important fact that many sports bettors overlook. Sports betting is not just about picking the winner; it is also about understanding how the public will bet and how that can affect the odds on the game.

892. Many times when a team is on a winning streak, bettors jump on the bandwagon and the line becomes inflated. Keep this in mind when you are analyzing the game. Many times the team on the winning streak will not cover the inflated point spread.

893. The same principle applies at the start of a new season. It is quite common to see the previous year's Super Bowl winner be a heavy favorite during the first few games of the next football season.

894. It is not uncommon to see point spreads of twenty or more for college games. Many of the collegiate teams cover these large spreads easily; they can and do often win by a large number of points, more so than pro teams. NFL point spreads tend to be much lower, in the three- to six-point range. It's unusual to see an NFL team favored by more than fourteen points.

895. Analyzing the point spreads can be particularly helpful in spotting potential upsets. Home-field advantage is worth about three points in the NFL and about six in college games. So, when you see an NFL team that's only a one- or two-point underdog on the road, you may have found an upset in the making. The same applies in college, where a team that's favored by less than six points may be headed for a loss when they play at home.

896. When you are betting football and basketball with the point spread laying 110 to win 100 on every bet, you need to win 52.38 percent of your bets just to break even. This is because you have to cover the vig charged by the sports book. The vig makes the house edge 4.5 percent on these bets.

897. One of the most popular and simplest betting strategies used by many players is to bet against the public. The logic is simple: always bet against the public. Simply bet against whichever team the public is loading up on. Look at the underdogs first for a line that may be inflated toward the favorite.

898. The value players employ a similar strategy, but the key difference is that they are always looking for betting line value. They watch line movement in the days leading up to the event to pinpoint lopsided wagering on one team. Heavy betting and money on one team will cause the betting line to move drastically. The value player then bets the opposite side.

899. A "square" or "sucker" line is a betting line designed by sports books to lure the public into heavily betting one way. This is also refereed to as a trap. Usually, if a line is too good to be true, then it's a sucker line. If Philadelphia has been winning their games by double digits and are now only a six-point favorite over Cleveland, it might be a trap.

900. Vary your bets. Don't bet the same amount on every game. If your information has one team heavily favored as compared to other games you are considering, then bet more on that game. If you bet two games for the same amount and you split, you will still lose because of the vig.

901. Bet with your head, not your heart. Too often sports bettors will not bet against their favorite team even when the facts clearly show they should. If you are the type of fan who can't bring yourself to bet against a favorite team, then you should avoid that game completely when you are choosing one to bet on.

14.

The Best Things in Life Are Free: Comps

902. The word comp is short for complimentary. Comps are freebies that the casino gives to its customers as a reward for their business; they are a marketing tool that casinos use to attract player loyalty. Comps are based on the theoretical amount that the casino figures it will win from a player. A portion of this win is returned to the player in the form of comps. You should try to get all the comps you are entitled to.

903. There is a misconception held by players that comps do not cost the casino anything, but they do. Food, drinks, and labor to supply the services cost the casino money. Displacing paying guests to supply a room for a comped player costs the casino money. Casinos establish comp policies to try to make it fair for the player and the casino alike.

Different Levels of Comps

904. Many players think that comps are only for the high rollers who spend thousands of dollars each visit, but this is not true. There are different levels of comps, depending on the amount of play you give the casinos. You should learn about the comp policy at the casinos where you play.

905. RFB stands for room, food, and beverage, which means your room, food, and drinks are all on the house. This comp is reserved for higher-level players. RLFB is the term used for room and limited food and beverage, which means your room is comped, but there is a dollar limit placed on the amount of food and drinks you can have for free. Casinos do this to protect themselves from players who might use more comps than their play entitles them to have.

906. Room comps will give the player a free room only, with no food or drinks added. If you stay at a casino and you only have a room comp, you still might be eligible for food and drinks based on your play. You can charge your meals to your hotel room and then ask a host to look at your play before you check out. If you qualify for additional comps, they will take some or all of your food charges off the bill.

907. Food comps are not too difficult to obtain. The casino will usually issue you a comp with a maximum dollar amount. If you go over your comp amount, you will have to pay the difference. Remember that gratuities are not included in you food comp, and it is your responsibility to take care of your server.

908. If you play table games, you can ask the pit boss for a breakfast or lunch comp at the table. If you do get one, it will not show up on your bill. You can then charge your dinner to your room and there is a good chance your food charges will be picked up because you only have one or two meals charged instead of all your meals.

909. Casino rate is a comp that is fairly easy to obtain if you don't qualify for a free room. The casinos like you staying and playing at their establishment. In return, they are willing to give you a discount on the room rate. Ask about casino rate when you book your room.

910. Entertainment comps will get you into the casino's shows for free. Some show tickets will be easier to obtain than others based on the popularity of the show. Casinos like to fill their showrooms. The best time to ask for a show comp is a few hours before the show. If it is not sold out, you will probably be able to get a seat from your casino host.

911. Line passes are comps that cost the casino nothing, but make the players happy. A line pass will let you go to the head of the line for the buffet, restaurant, or a show. All you have to do is ask a pit boss or casino host for a line pass. I have yet to be denied one of these comps when I asked.

912. Free drinks are the universal comp that is given to all players. Most casinos serve you free drinks while you are playing at the slots or table games. Be careful if you drink alcohol when you play. Drinking too much alcohol can cause you to lose your inhibitions and bet more than you intended.

913. Funbooks are little booklets of coupons handed out by the casino. They contain coupons for gambling, dining, souvenirs, discounts, and gift offers. Ask for them at the players club or welcome booth.

914. Match play coupons or lucky bucks are often found in the casino funbooks. They give you additional money if you win a bet at the table games. For example, if you have a five dollar match play coupon, you can bet five dollars with the coupon and if you win, you will be paid ten dollars.

915. Double points is another comp offered by the casino. During a certain time or on a given day, the casino will double all the points you earn on your player's card. These promotions are usually aimed at the slot machine players. It is definitely worth your while to play during double point times, especially if the casino offers cash back for your play.

916. Cash back is one of the best comps because you receive cold hard cash for your play. When a casino offers cash back, you usually redeem a certain number of player's points for a dollar amount. For example, a casino might give you five dollars for every 2,500 points on your player's card.

917. Mailers are sent out by the casino marketing department to players from time to time. Many of the mailers will contain some sort of offer to entice you to visit the casino and play. While many of these offers are useless, some occasionally contain something of value. Read the mailer instead of just tossing it out with your junk mail.

918. Promotional gifts are offered by many casinos for members of their players club; they might be sent to you for your birthday or anniversary or a monthly giveaway. You are required to pick up your gift in person. Often players will lose more than the gift is worth when they go to pick it up.

919. Casinos extend invitations to special events as a form of comp for their good players. These might include free slot tournaments, shows, or other events being held. You should consider the cost of getting to these events and find out what else is included before accepting an invitation.

Comp Basics

920. The casino will usually require you to play three to four hours a day to qualify for the higher end comps. The casino figures your theoretical loss and then gives you back a percentage of your loss in comps. It doesn't matter if you are playing table games or the machine games; they just want you to have your money at risk.

921. The basic formula for figuring your rating is: (average bet size) x (hours played) x (hands per hour) x (house advantage) = theoretical loss. In a game of blackjack, you may see seventy-five hands per hour and the casino figures to have a 2 percent edge over the average player. If you bet ten dollars per hand and played for four hours, they would figure your loss as sixty dollars ($10 x 4 hours x 75 hph x .02 = $60).

922. When you use your player's card, you win even if you lose. You might have a losing session at the tables or while playing the machines, but you are getting something back in the way of comps when you use your player's card or get rated at the table.

923. No one will come up to you and ask if you would like a comp. You will have to ask for the comp that you want. If your play qualifies for the comp you are looking for, you will get it. If not, you can ask how much play is required for that comp. The most important thing to remember when looking for a comp is that you have to ask. Just be sure that you ask politely and thank the person who gives you the comp.

924. If you are looking for a food comp, it is best to do this while you are playing. If you are playing the machines, you will need to speak to a casino host. You can tell one of the slot attendants that you would like to speak to a casino host and ask them to page one for you. If you are playing the tables, you can ask the pit boss.

925. Never play at a higher limit or for a longer period of time just to obtain a comp. In many instances you will lose more money than if you had just purchased the meal or show outright.

926. Don't get greedy. If you receive a comp to a restaurant, don't run up the bill by ordering a lot of expensive food you don't really want. If you do, you may find that you will not get another comp the next time you ask.

Players Clubs

927. The slot clubs and players clubs originated in Atlantic City. The majority of casino customers were day trippers who arrived on buses. Casino execs quickly realized that unless their best customers were recognized and rewarded, they could easily walk next door to another casino. In 1982, the Galaxy Slot Club debuted at the Sands; the other casinos were quick to start their own clubs to capitalize on player loyalty.

928. Most casinos have players clubs to keep track of your play. This is how they determine what comps you are entitled to. You should always join the players club. It is free to join and many clubs have a free gift or other incentives for joining. It is very important to shop around and play at the casinos that offer the best club benefits along with the best games. If you find yourself at a small casino without a players club, I would not give them much play.

929. Being a member of the players club can get you a room when the hotel is booked. Some casinos reserve a few rooms for their club members at busy times of the year. At some casinos, just being a member of the club will entitle you to casino rate.

930. Never put a single coin in a machine or play a hand at the tables without using your player's card. If you don't use your card, you are essentially giving away free money because the comps you receive from the casino have value. In some casinos you are eligible for casino rate if you have a player's card with any amount of play on it, so once you get it, be sure to at least put a few dollars of play on it.

931. To sign up for a player's card, fill out an application at the club's booth in the casino. Be sure to bring photo identification. The application form usually has spaces for you to fill in your birthday and anniversary dates, so the marketing department can send you offers on your special day. They may also ask for your social security number, but in this day and age of identity theft, I urge you not to fill it in.

932. Some couples prefer to maintain separate players club accounts. One advantage is that each member may receive separate offers for special events. On the other hand, if you sign up for a joint account, your play will be added together and you may be eligible for more comps than you would earn individually.

933. Many casinos are installing comp kiosks where a player can comp themselves based on the points they have earned on the player's card. You put your card in the kiosk, and it will display your available comp benefits. If you want a restaurant comp, you put in the amount you would like, and it will print your comp right on the spot.

934. Always have a casino host evaluate your play before you check out. You might qualify for a few free nights or a reduction of your hotel and food bill. If you don't have a host, call the hotel operator and ask to be connected to a casino host.

Slot Machines

935. Comps for slot and video poker players are based on the amount of money you play through the machine during a given period. When you replay coins you have won, it counts as money being played. The money you replay is referred to as "churn."

936. Some players refuse to use their player's card in the slot machines because they think they lose when they use it. There is no link between the card reader and the random number generator in the machine. You will lose more in the way of comps by not using your card.

937. When you sign up for your player's card, you can ask for a second card. When you sit down and play, put your second card in the machine next to you. Play a coin or two and then "forget" to take your card out. Many players don't use their card and if they sit down and play at that machine, you may get credit for it.

938. If you see a player sitting next to you who is not using a card, ask him if he forgot to put his card in. If he says he doesn't use a card, ask to put your extra card in his machine. You then get credit for his play as well as your own.

939. Table game players need to get their play rated every time they sit down at a table game. Put your player's card on the table when you buy into the game. The floor supervisor will pick it up and start a rating slip for you.

940. Your rating for table game play is based on several factors. The length of time you play, the size of your average bet, and the amount of money that you buy in with are all considered when determining your rating. The casino then figures out your theoretical loss and gives you back a percentage. Buying in for more will get you a slightly higher rating. If you have the discipline not to get carried away, you should buy in for more money than you actually plan to risk.

941. Keep your experience a secret. Acting like a knowledgeable player and giving advice to other players is a sure way to lower your comp level. Casinos give more comps to players they think don't know how to play properly.

942. One way to increase your rating is to make a slightly larger bet when you first sit down at the table. Do this when the floor supervisor is picking up your players card. They usually only watch your first few bets when you enter the game. Making larger bets to start will usually get you a higher rating.

943. When you sit down at the table, it might take a few minutes for the pit boss to pick up your card. Some players will sit and wait before making their first bet to make sure they get all their rating time. It is better to just mention to the pit boss that you have been in for a few hands if it takes time for them to get to you.

944. If you ask for a comp when you are playing a table game, the pit boss will take time to "check" your play. They are really hoping to get you to play a few more hands while they are processing your comp. You are not obligated to play.

945. A good strategy is to ask for your comp a few minutes before you plan to stop playing. This way you do not end up playing longer than you had planned to. The pit boss will think she has enticed you to play a few more hands when, in reality, you are not playing any longer than you wanted to.

946. Another way to get your comp faster is to quit playing once you ask. If you are just sitting at the table and not betting, they want to make that seat available to another player. Tell the dealer to color up your chips and then sit and wait for your comp.

15.

Safety Counts: Protecting Yourself and Your Money

947. If everyone were as honest as you and me, we would never have to worry about safety. Unfortunately, whenever there is money involved, you are bound to run into some dishonest people. Casinos do their best to protect the players and themselves from the criminal element with surveillance cameras and a large security force; however, we must also take it upon ourselves to help ensure our own safety. Always be vigilant in the casino.

948. Many men carry their wallets in their back pockets. This makes it easier for a nimble-fingered pickpocket to snatch. Carry your wallet in the front pocket and, better yet, wrap a rubber band around it. This will make it more difficult to lift from your pocket.

949. Purses, cameras, and other valuables should never be placed on the shelf between the slot machines. You could easily forget them or someone could reach over from the other side of the slot bank and grab them. Keep your purse on your shoulder or set it on your lap while you play.

950. The use of a fanny pack is quite common by both genders of casino patrons. Most of these are worn on the person's side. While they are convenient for holding sunglasses, player's cards, and other incidentals, you should never carry money, wallets, or other valuables in them. The pack's straps can easily be cut, and a thief can quickly make off with it.

951. When you feed a bill into the receptor of the slot machine, make sure you watch it go into the machine. Sometimes the receptor will spit the bill back out if it is crinkled or inserted wrong. If you look away when the bill comes back out, a quick thief can snatch it, leaving you to wonder why the credits did not register on your machine.

952. Beware of the bump from a stranger. Many pickpockets work in teams. One thief will bump you and the other will lift your wallet. If you do get bumped, you should immediately reach for your wallet to make sure that it is still there.

953. When you get paid at the cashier's cage, take a minute to put your money into your pocket or purse. Don't walk away from the cage with stacks of dollar bills in your hand. There is no need to advertise that you have money.

954. Always count your change before you leave the cashier's window. If a mistake was made, it will be too late to correct once you walk away. Don't worry if there is a line behind you; take a minute to make sure you received the correct amount.

955. If you should win a large hand-paid jackpot, you can ask to have a security guard walk you to the cage. If you are staying at the casino, you should put the money in the safe deposit box that most casinos make available to hotel guests. If you are traveling by car, you can ask security to walk you to your vehicle to make sure you get there safely.

956. Most casinos offer valet parking, and at some casinos, it is free. Even if you have to pay, it is worth the cost for your safety. If you are planning to play into the wee hours of the morning or just want some added safety, valet is the way to go.

957. Never get into an elevator with someone who makes you feel nervous. You can always wait a minute for the next car. Your personal safety comes first and waiting a few extra minutes for a different elevator is worth it if only for your own peace of mind.

958. When riding in an elevator, try to stand against the back wall or either side of the car. This gives you a clear view of everyone in the car and helps protect you against someone lifting your wallet.

959. You should always carry emergency identification on you in a place other than your wallet or purse. (This is not just for trips to casinos; it is a good practice to do this whenever you are traveling.) If you should become unconscious and have your wallet or purse stolen, there is still a way to be identified. Even keeping your player's card in a different pocket will help to identify you in an emergency.

960. Some hotel room doors close slowly. When you enter or leave your hotel room, you should push or pull the door shut. Make sure that it locks before you walk away.

961. Don't carry all your money with you. Take only enough money for your playing session or night out. Keep the rest locked in your room safe or the hotel safe. This will also keep you from spending more that you planned to.

962. When traveling, you should avoid carrying large amounts of cash. Convert your money into traveler's checks or bring an ATM card. You can replace these if they are lost or stolen.

963. Don't carry buckets of coins to and from your room. It is much safer to cash them in at the casino cage. Besides being cumbersome and easy to spill, they advertise that you have money left in your room. Carrying coins is advertisement of the wrong kind.

964. If you are too tired to pay attention to your game or your surroundings, stop playing. When you are tired, you can drop or lose chips. You may also find yourself making larger bets than you planned.

965. Avoid drinking too much alcohol while you are playing. A tipsy player becomes a prime candidate for unscrupulous people. If you have a drink in the lounge after playing, never leave your drink unattended where it can be tampered with.

966. Slot players should not play more machines than they can easily reach. If you are not playing one of the coinless machines, a passerby could easily take coins from your tray.

967. Stay seated at your machine if you hit a jackpot or need a hopper fill when you are cashing out. Some players will leave the machine and go looking for a slot attendant. This makes it possible for someone to jump in and claim that they were playing the machine.

968. Table game players should keep track of their chips. Some casinos require you to leave chips on the table when you take a bathroom break. Take a quick count before you get up. If possible, take the majority with you and leave a small portion on the table to hold your spot.

969. Craps players are required to keep their chips in the rail. Put smaller denomination chips on both sides of your stack, keeping the larger chips in the middle. Stand close to them and put you hand over the top if you suspect a nearby player.

970. Men should be wary if a drop-dead gorgeous woman approaches them. Before you start to flatter yourself about your irresistible charm, you better face reality. She might be a prostitute. The casinos are not the only ones trying to separate you from your money.

971. Men should use the stall in the men's room. When you are standing at the urinal, an attacker can sneak up behind you and grab you around the neck in a stranglehold.

Cheating and Scams

972. Casinos in most states are governed by a regulatory agency. To ensure the integrity of their staffs, casino personnel are screened and must pass a background check. This is not the case in all states and some foreign countries. Don't gamble in jurisdictions with inadequate regulations.

973. Casinos are a billion-dollar industry. If they are caught cheating the customers, they would be closed down by the state regulators. The casinos do everything possible to ensure that players are not being cheated. They have an edge on all the games, so there is no need for them to cheat.

974. Most casinos prohibit their employees from playing in the casino where they work. In some jurisdictions, it is a law. This is to help prevent theft by employees, which makes up a major portion of all casino theft. Dealers are required to clap and show their hands when they leave a table so the surveillance cameras can see they are not pocketing chips.

975. Everybody makes mistakes, and dealers are no exception. If you feel a mistake has been made or suspect that you have been cheated, ask to speak to the pit boss. They can review the play by calling the "eye in the sky" to check the tapes.

976. The casinos spend millions of dollars trying to thwart scams by players who are trying to cheat. The casino security departments have seen just about every form of cheating attempted by players. You would have to be pretty foolish to think you could get away with it.

977. Remember the old adage, "If it sounds too good to be true, it probably is!" Don't fall for scams by con artists. If you are approached by someone with a surefire way to get rich in the casino, walk away as quickly as you can.

16.

Thanks for the Tip: Who, When, and How Much to Tip

978. Dealers are part of the service industry, as are waitresses and bartenders. Most of their income is derived from tips, so don't forget to tip them for good service. The best way to do this is to make a bet for them. This makes the dealers feel as if they are in the game with you, and they'll be rooting for you to win.

979. While tipping the dealer is customary, you don't want to over-tip. If you are playing a negative expectation game, you are going to lose money in the long run. If you over-tip, it could mean the difference between a small win and a small loss.

980. The best way to tip a craps dealer is to make a bet for him or her on the pass line. This bet has a better chance of winning than making one of the proposition bets. Just put a dollar chip on the pass line next to your bet and tell them it is for the dealer. Even if the table has a five-dollar minimum, you are allowed to bet less than that when it is a dealer tip.

981. When your bet for the dealer wins, the dealer will take the winnings and the original tip bet. A better way to tip is to place the dollar tip on top of your bet. When it wins, give the dealer the winning chip, but keep the original dollar on your bet. If you have a winning streak, the dealer will get more.

982. Poker dealers rely on tips, as do other casino dealers. During a live game, it is customary for the winner of the pot to tip the dealer. Usually a player will tip the dealer a dollar a pot. In some low-limit games, the player may opt for fifty cents, but most players will tip something when they win.

983. When you have a jackpot that requires a hand pay by the attendant, it is customary to tip them when they bring you your money. Again, this is based on the service received. If the jackpot was paid quickly, a tip is in order. Usually a tip of .5 percent to 1 percent of the jackpot is considered fair, so you might give five or ten dollars on a thousand dollar jackpot.

984. If you have a handpaid jackpot, you will usually be paid with large bills. The attendants are hoping you will be so happy with your win that you will give them a twenty-dollar bill or more. You should carry a few five or ten dollar bills to use for tipping the attendants on your jackpot.

985. There are usually two or three people in attendance during a hand pay. This is for security reasons to make sure the correct amount of money is being paid to the correct person. You don't have to tip each attendant separately. You can give one person a larger bill and tell them to split it.

986. Some slot attendants will watch or hold a machine for you while you take a bathroom break. In some casinos, you can have the attendant lock up your machine while you go for a meal. If you ask an attendant to do this for you, it is customary to give them a dollar or two when you return.

987. Casino hosts are not allowed to accept cash tips, as this would appear to be a conflict of interest. They are allowed to accept small gifts from you. I generally will give ties or golf balls for the male hosts and a scarf or flowers to the female hosts.

988. One of the best tips you can give any casino employee is a letter sent to their boss. In the letter give the employee's name and a short description of the fine service the employee gave or how helpful he or she was. You can easily learn the name of the casino manager or shift supervisor by asking.

989. You should always tip your beverage server at least one dollar for each drink. Because their tips are part of their salary, some casinos require the waitress or waiter to pay a tax on each drink they order to take out onto the casino floor. If you order a drink and leave before it is delivered or you don't tip the server, you have just cost them money.

Other Tipping

990. Tipping in a restaurant is the same everywhere—usually 15 to 20 percent of the total bill. If you have a comped meal, you should still tip your server. Tips are not covered in the comp.

991. Many casino bars have slot machines built into the bar tops that you can play while seated at the bar. Many casinos give free drinks if you play the machines. You should give the bartender at least a dollar per drink, the same as you would the waitress on the casino floor.

992. Many people feel that since a buffet is self-service, a tip is not required. Usually a server gets your drinks or takes away your dirty dishes. You should leave a dollar for each person eating at your table.

993. You should always tip a bellhop who assists you with your luggage. The customary tip is a dollar a bag with a minimum of three dollars. Small hand-held ladies cosmetic cases, men's briefcases, and kids' plush toys do not count. Count large athletic equipment bags or golf club bags as one and a half.

994. You can sometimes get a room with a better view or a slightly better room if you tip the front desk clerk. When you get to the counter, it often works to casually slide a folded twenty-dollar bill on the counter at the same time as making a request for a special room or even a free upgrade.

995. You should tip the hotel house cleaners a couple of dollars per night when you check out. In most hotels, there is a card in the room with the name of your house cleaner. You can place your tip by the card. I have found it is better to look for your house cleaner and hand him or her the tip personally.

996. Some casinos offer free shuttles to and from the airport in a bus or limo. Five or ten dollars is usually considered an average tip for the drive. Based on the amount of bags you have, you may want to give more.

997. At the car rental booth, you may be able to get an upgrade for a twenty-dollar tip. Slide the folded bill across the counter and ask the desk clerk if there are any specials or upgrades available. You can sometimes get a bigger car at a lower daily rate.

998. Valet parking is free at many casinos. You should tip the attendant at least two dollars. You usually tip when you pick up your car. If you have a special request, such as keeping your car parked close by for a quicker exit, then you should tip when you drop it off as well.

999. You are not obligated to tip anyone. If you receive poor service or your server has been rude or offensive, you should not leave a tip. If you wish, you can tell the server why you are not leaving a tip so they know it was because of poor service and not that you forgot.

1000. Every person I know likes to be appreciated and praised when he or she does a good job. A simple compliment can be a form of tipping. It costs nothing and pays back tremendous dividends.

Appendix

Problem Gambling

The casino is an exciting place to be. Some players take the time to learn the skills needed to play the games with the primary goal of winning money, but the majority of players visit the casino for entertainment. Playing the games is an enjoyable experience and the lure of winning money adds to the excitement. Some players enjoy the adrenaline rush that accompanies the thrill of risking their money on the games. For some, this high can be seductive and alluring and a small number of players succumb to the darker side of gambling—addiction.

An addiction is a compulsive need. Some people become addicted to alcohol, drugs, sex, or food, and the problem can be just as serious with gambling. What starts as a pleasurable experience turns into a destructive, uncontrollable craving. When the thrill of the game outweighs everything else, the player has crossed over the line from player to addict. As with any addiction, gambling can be devastating for addicts and the people close to them.

Gamblers Anonymous uses a list of twenty questions to help players determine whether they may have a gambling problem. I urge you to take a moment to read through the list of questions and answer them honestly.

1. Did you ever lose time from work or school due to gambling?
2. Has gambling ever made your home life unhappy?
3. Did gambling affect your reputation?
4. Have you ever felt remorse after gambling?
5. Did you ever gamble to get money with which to pay debts or otherwise solve financial difficulties?
6. Did gambling cause a decrease in your ambition or efficiency?
7. After losing, did you feel you must return as soon as possible and win back your losses?
8. After a win, did you have a strong urge to return and win more?
9. Did you often gamble until your last dollar was gone?
10. Did you ever borrow to finance your gambling?
11. Have you ever sold anything to finance gambling?
12. Were you reluctant to use "gambling money" for normal expenditures?
13. Did gambling make you careless of the welfare of yourself or your family?
14. Did you ever gamble longer than you had planned?

15. Have you ever gambled to escape worry or trouble?
16. Have you ever committed, or considered committing, an illegal act to finance gambling?
17. Did gambling cause you to have difficulty sleeping?
18. Do arguments, disappointments, or frustrations create within you an urge to gamble?
19. Did you ever have an urge to celebrate any good fortune by a few hours of gambling?
20. Have you ever considered self-destruction or suicide because of your gambling?

Most compulsive gamblers will answer yes to at least seven of these questions.

Sometimes people think they may have a problem and after they read the questions, they realize that they do. If you or someone you love has a problem, there are resources available no matter where you live. Please call the National Council on Problem Gambling hotline at 1-800-522-4700, or contact Gambler's Anonymous by calling (213) 386-8789. You can also visit their website at www.gamblersanonymous.org.

Additional Resources

There is a wealth of resources available for any player who would like to learn more about casinos and casino games. There are books, tutorial software programs, Internet websites, and even live seminars to help you learn. Here are some of the resources I recommend.

Books

• *Blackjack: Take the Money and Run*
  by Henry Tamburin

This is a clear and easy-to-understand book that will take the reader from basic blackjack strategy for the novice player to more advanced card counting techniques.

• *Knock-Out Blackjack: The Easiest Card-Counting System Ever Devised* by Vancura and Fuchs

This book teaches a simple, unbalanced counting system. It is very easy to understand.

• *The Frugal Gambler and More Frugal Gambling*
  by Jean Scott

Jean Scott is the Queen of Comps. Both of her books will teach every aspect of the comp game and how to get more than your share at the casino.

• *Video Poker: Optimum Play* by Dan Paymar

This book covers all the aspects of video poker including how to play and bankroll considerations. It concentrates on jacks or better, deuces wild, and jokers wild.

• *Get the Edge at Low-Limit Texas Hold'em*
  by Bill Burton

My book will teach you how to play winning low limit Texas hold'em. The book is written in an easy-to-understand style. It is designed for the novice player who wants to learn how to play the game properly.

- *The Theory of Poker* by David Sklansky
If you want to be a winning poker player, you have to understand the basic concepts of the game. This book teaches you the theory behind the strategy.

- *The Golden Touch Dice Control Revolution!*
  by Frank Scoblete
Learn dice control with the most advanced book on the subject. Over seventy photographs will show you everything you need to know to get the edge over the casinos in the game of craps.

- *Sports Betting 101: Making Sense of the Bookie Business and the Business of Beating the Bookie*
  by Arne Lang
An excellent book for anyone who wants to learn about sports betting and specific strategies for all sporting events. It includes an informal history of bookmaking.

- *The Unofficial Guide to Casino Gambling*
  by Basil Nester
One of the best all-around general gambling books covering all the casino games. Written in an easy-to-understand and informative manner.

Tutorial Software Programs

- Blackjack 6-7-8 by Sticky Soft
  www.blackjack678.com
  Blackjack 6-7-8 is one of the best blackjack software programs on the market. It will train you in basic strategy and card counting. You can also run high-speed simulations. It does everything that other software does at half the price.

- Bob Dancer Presents WinPoker
  by Zamzow Software Solutions
  www.zamzone.com
  This video poker tutorial program teaches you the correct way to play any video poker game. It has a built-in tutor, lets you change the pay table, and analyzes any game or hand.

- Frugal Video Poker by Jim Wolf
  www.frugalgambler.biz
  This video poker software is the next generation in tutorial software. It not only teaches you how to play the game, it also lets you print out strategy charts to take with you.

- Wilson Poker Software
  www.wilsonsoftware.com
  Wilson makes the absolute best poker tutorial software. There are separate software programs available for Texas hold'em, 7-card stud, Omaha, and tournament play.

Seminars

- Golden Touch Craps
  www.goldentouchcraps.com
  Golden Touch Craps teaches a hands-on seminar for precision craps shooting and dice setting. In the two-day seminar, you learn the eight physical elements of precision shooting and the skills needed to be an advanced craps player.
- Golden Touch Blackjack
  www.goldentouchblackjack.com
  Golden Touch Blackjack teaches the revolutionary speed count. It is the easiest blackjack card counting method to learn. Speed count is taught exclusively at the seminar and not published in any book.

The Internet

- About.com Casino Gambling
  www.casinogambling.about.com
  You can learn more about casino gambling here or contact me directly at my website www.bill-burton.com.

Glossary

Across the board: To bet on a horse to finish first (win), finish second (place), or finish third (show).

Board: The community cards in poker. It is also the area in the sports book where the games and lines are posted.

Bust: To go over the total of twenty-one in black-jack. If you go over twenty-one, you lose. If the dealer goes over twenty-one and you have not, you win. If the player and dealer both bust, the player still loses.

Blinds: The large and small blinds are forced bets made in Texas hold'em before the first cards are dealt.

Bluff: To bet or raise in poker with an inferior hand in an attempt to make the other players fold, allow-ing the bluffer to win the pot.

Buy in: To exchange your cash for chips when you play a casino table game.

Call: In poker, to place money in the pot equal to the previous bet.

Calling station: A weak, passive player who will not fold his hand and will call until the last card is dealt. A calling station rarely raises the pot, but you will make the most money from this type of player.

Card counting: In blackjack, a method by which a player keeps track of the high and low cards dealt to gain an edge over the casino.

Casino rate: This is a reduced hotel rate given to players who are good customers, but do not play enough to qualify for a free room.

Check: To decline to bet during a round of poker. You can only check if no one has bet before it is your turn to act.

Check raise: To check (not bet) your poker hand and then raise after another player has bet.

Come bet: In craps, this bet is similar to a pass line bet, but it is made after a point is established.

Come out: In craps, this is the initial roll made by a new shooter to establish a point.

Comp: Short for "complimentary." It is a reward given to good customers that may include free rooms, show tickets, meals, and more.

Don't bet: This craps bet is made when the player is betting against the shooter.

Double down: To double your bet after receiving your first two cards in blackjack. After this point, the dealer will give you only one more card.

Drop: All the casino's receipts from a table game.

Even money: Winning an amount equal to the original wager. On an even money bet, if you bet ten dollars, you would retain your original ten-dollar bet, plus be paid an additional ten dollars.

Expected value or EV: The percentage of the total money wagered that a player could expect to win or lose on any bet.

Eye in the sky: Surveillance cameras mounted in the ceiling of the casino that allow security to monitor all activity in the casino.

First base: The first player spot at the blackjack table immediately to the dealer's left. The first person to be dealt cards in blackjack.

Flop: In Texas hold'em, the flop is the first three community cards turned over by the dealer.

Fold: To cease play by throwing in your hand.

Four to a flush: In video poker when a player's hand contains four of the five cards needed for a royal flush.

Hand: In poker, it is the five cards the player uses to make the best poker combination. In blackjack, a hand is the cards dealt to the player.

Hard hand: A blackjack hand that does not contain an Ace.

Hardway: This is a bet in the center of the craps layout in which you are betting on the dice showing as a pair to make four (two and two), six (three and three), eight (four and four) or ten (five and five).

Hedge: To make two offsetting bets in the hopes that one will win and give the bettor a small profit.

High hand: In pai gow, the high hand is made up of five cards. This hand must have a higher poker value than the two-card hand, which is called the second high hand.

Hit: The term used in blackjack to indicate that the player wants to draw another card.

Hole card: Cards that are dealt face down. In blackjack, it is the dealer's face-down card. In poker, it is the cards dealt face down to the players.

House edge: The difference between the true odds and the amount of money that the casino actually pays the player when she wins. The casino makes its money by paying the player a little less than true odds when he or she wins a bet.

Inside bet: In roulette, it is a bet made on one or more of the numbers on the layout. In craps, it is a place bet made on the five, six, eight, or nine.

Insurance: In blackjack, the player can make a side bet on whether or not the dealer has a natural blackjack when the dealer has an Ace showing.

Kicker: An unpaired high card in your hand used to break a tie in poker. Kickers should never be held when playing video poker.

Line: A handicap assigned to a favored sporting team to make the underdog more attractive to bettors.

Marker: A marker is essentially a loan from the casino. Once a player establishes a line of credit with the casino, he is allowed to take a marker, which he must pay back within a certain time.

Martingale: A dangerous system of doubling the bet every time the wager loses.

Outside bet: In roulette, it is any of the bets made on the outside of the layout that does not contain the individual numbers. In craps, it is a bet on the four and ten.

Pass: The term used in craps when the shooter throws a seven or eleven on the come out roll or makes his point and wins.

Pass line: The area on the craps layout where a player places his bet when he is betting that the shooter will win.

Pass line bet: This craps bet is made when the player is betting with the shooter. (See also pass line.)

Parlay: To double your bet when you win. In sports betting, it is the term for betting on multiple games in a single bet. In a parlay bet, all of the games bet on need to win for the bettor to collect.

Place bet: In craps, it is making a bet on the craps layout on the four, five, six, eight, nine, or ten. In horse racing, it is betting on a horse to come in second.

Point: In craps, this is the number rolled by the shooter on the come out roll. It will be four, five, six, eight, nine, or ten. The shooter must roll the number again before rolling a seven in order to win.

Point spread: One form of handicap used to make two sporting teams equally attractive to the betting public.

Probability: The mathematical likelihood of an event occurring. It is expressed as a percentage or a number between zero and one.

Proposition or prop bets: These are wagers on the bets in the center of the craps layout that include the hardway bets and the one-roll bets. They all have a high house edge.

Roll: To toss the dice in a craps game. The term "on a roll" is used to describe a winning streak.

River: The fifth and last community card turned over by the dealer in a Texas hold'em game.

Semi-bluff: To bet or raise in poker with a hand that you think is not the best hand, but has a reasonable chance of improving to the best hand.

Seven out: The term used when a craps player rolls a seven before making their point. The player loses and the dice are passed to the next shooter.

Shoe: The device used to hold the multiple decks of cards in a blackjack or baccarat game.

Show: Betting on a horse to come in third.

Slow play: When you play a strong poker hand weakly in hopes of getting more people to put money in the pot because raising would make other players fold.

Soft hand: A hand in blackjack that contains an Ace where the Ace can be counted as eleven, without going over twenty-one.

Split: In blackjack, the player is allowed to split a pair into two hands by placing an additional bet equal to the original bet on the second hand. The two hands are then played independently.

Stand: In blackjack, the player stands when he does not wish to take any additional cards. He indicates this to the dealer by waving his hand over his own cards.

Standard deviation: The fluctuation that occurs between the probability of an event occurring and the actual outcome.

Suited: In Texas hold'em, if a player's two hole cards are the same suit, they are suited. If all three cards of the flop are the same suit, it is called a suited flop.

Third base: The last seat to be dealt cards in a blackjack game. This is the last person to act before the dealer.

True odds: The actual probability that an event will occur.

Turn: The fourth community card turned over by the dealer in a Texas hold'em game.

Vigorish or vig: The fee or commission the casino collects on losing sports bets.

Virtual stops: The slot machine reels may have twenty-two symbols on each reel. These are the physical stops. Computer technology allows the slot machine to have 256 or more virtual stops, which are linked to one of the symbols on the physical reel.

Win: To make a successful wager. In horse racing, it is betting on a horse to come in first place.

Index

B

C

V

About the Author

Bill Burton is the Casino Gambling columnist for About.com (www.casinogambling.about.com) and author of *Get the Edge at Low Limit Texas Hold'em*.

He writes for several national gaming magazines and newsletters, including *The Southern California Gaming Guide, Midwest Gaming and Travel* magazine, *Southern Gaming and Destinations* magazine, and *The Crapshooter Newsletter.*

Mr. Burton is a certified instructor for Golden Touch Craps International and a regular speaker at the Frank Scoblete Gamblers Jamborees that have been held in several gaming destinations throughout the United States and Canada. He lives in New Britain, Connecticut.